JACOBUS REVIUS

SELECTED POEMS

JACOBUS REVIUS

DUTCH METAPHYSICAL POET

a parallel Dutch | English edition

S E L E C T E D   P O E M S

translated and with an introduction by

HENRIETTA TEN HARMSEL *Calvin College*

Wayne State University Press   Detroit   1968

CONTENTS

ACKNOWLEDGMENTS

I wish to thank the American Association of University Women for the Shirley Farr Fellowship, which provided my year in Utrecht, and Calvin College for granting me the leave to accept it; the staff at the Deventer Library for the permission to use and photograph their valuable documents; and the Uitgevers-Maatschappij Holland for the permission to reproduce Revius' poems from the *Over-Ysselsche Sangen en Dichten*.

For more personal help I am grateful to X. J. Kennedy, James S. Holmes, Jacob Vander Starre, Ruth Vande Kieft, John Mulder, and Stanley Wiersma for criticizing various drafts of my translations and introduction; to Professor Austin Warren for the inspiration to begin my work with Revius; and above all to Professor W. A. P. Smit — perceptive critic and gracious gentleman — for his constant encouragement, detailed direction, and wise counsel.

HENRIETTA TEN HARMSEL
UTRECHT, 1966

OVER-YSSELSCHE
SANGEN
EN
DICHTEN.
IACOBI REVII.

Pſalm: 146. verſ: 2.

Ick wil den Heere loben ſoo lange als ick leve/
ende mijnen God lof-ſingen dewijle
ick hier ben.

TOT DEVENTER.
Bij Sebaſtiaen Wermbouts/ Boeckdzucker woo-
nende op den Poot/ inden Vergulden Bijbel.

ANNO M. DC. XXX.

*The original title page of 1630 Dutch Edition
of the Poems of Jacobus Revius*

INTRODUCTION

The great painters of the Netherlands are universally known and admired. Rembrandt — Vermeer — Hals — these names are recognized by all lovers of art. But who knows the name of Revius? Or even the name of Vondel? Although the dark grandeur of a drama by Vondel is comparable to that of a painting by Rembrandt; although the subtle symbolism of a sonnet by Revius is comparable to that of a scene by Vermeer; still the world has learned to know the painters, but not the poets. That is the reason for the translations in this volume. They can be only reproductions, it is true. But many people have learned to know Rembrandt and Vermeer only through reproductions. With a sense of hope and humility, then, I present these poetic reproductions of Revius. With humility, because the translation of a poem inevitably loses more of its original than does the reproduction of a painting. With hope, because even with their glory diminished, Revius' poems are well worth reading.

REVIUS AND HIS BACKGROUND

Jacobus Revius (1586–1658) was very much a part of the golden age of the Netherlands. When the Spanish occupied his birthplace, Deventer, in 1586, he was forced in his infancy to flee with his mother to Amsterdam. Thus the determined resistance against Spanish domination and the fervent struggle for independence which united the Netherlands and prepared for its golden age were practi-

9

cally born into his blood. Ardently Calvinist by birth and scrupulously trained in Reformed theology and the history of the Christian church, Revius was a part of the vigorous Protestantism which produced the Synod of Dordt in 1619 and the authorized Staten-Bijbel in 1637. Thoroughly educated in classical languages and literature, he sought both to apply and transcend the rich ideals of Renaissance humanism by seeing them recreated, redeemed, and sanctified in a God-centered universe. Deeply concerned with the cultural development of his native city, he recorded its history in Latin in his *Daventria Illustrata* and helped his townsmen establish the Athenaeum school, its library, and a music college in Deventer. But more than any of these, his poetry makes Revius a part of his exciting century. His patriotism and his Protestantism; his baroque sensibility and his metaphysical mind; his knowledge of the ancient classics, the church fathers, and the French Renaissance; above all, his personal, Calvinistic, artistic, and spiritual comprehension of the Word of God — all of these inform his *Over-Ysselsche Sangen en Dichten*, his unique contribution to world poetry.

In spite of the variety and volume of his poetry, Revius was long known chiefly as a theologian. Trained for the ministry at the University of Leiden, he devoted himself to the Reformed Church: as pastor at Deventer from 1614–1642; as adviser to scholarship students in theology at Leiden from 1642–1658; as contributor to the translation of the *Staten-Bijbel*; as originator of an improved versification of the Psalms; and as writer of many and varied scholarly theological works, including controversial pamphlets against the Remonstrants and the Cartesians, translations of the *Netherlands Confession of Faith* into Greek and Latin, and Protestant adaptations of various classic studies in theology.

Revius' own century and the two succeeding centuries

continued to stress his theological work much more than his poetry. The 1630 publication of his poems and its expanded version in 1634 gained a somewhat limited success. Only scattered examples of his poems appeared during the following centuries in anthologies or small selected editions. A thesis by E. Meyjes in 1895 still emphasized Revius' work in theology although it included a closing section on his poetry. It was chiefly the work of Professor W. A. P. Smit — his admirable study of Revius' poetry in 1928 and his definitive editions of the poems in 1930 and 1935 — that brought about the great revival of Revius in this century. Since then, many critical articles have been written on his poetry, he has become generally accepted as the leading Calvinist lyric poet of his country, and his name has been mentioned with the other well-known baroque and metaphysical poets of his age.

Although Revius was not an active member of the literary circles of his time, his poetry naturally reflects connections with that of his Dutch contemporaries. The homely moralizing of the popular Jacob Cats; the song-like quality of the poems of Pieter C. Hooft; the epigrammatic and witty tendencies of Constantijn Huygens, who translated some of Donne's poetry into Dutch; especially the poetic eulogies on Dutch heroes and the dignified vernacular and baroque splendor of the *Lof-Sanck van Jesus Christus* by Daniel Heinsius, the famed classicist and Calvinist poet whom Revius greatly admired — all of these find echoes in the *Over-Ysselsche Sangen en Dichten*. Foreign influences on Revius are even more marked: the Odes of Horace and Pindar; the Idylls of Theocritus; the vast body of Scriptural explication by the church fathers; the Protestant poetry of Du Bartas; the Latin epigrams of the English John Owen; above all, the poetry of Ronsard, from whom Revius adapted much in style and form. Undoubtedly, his participation in the baroque spirit — and that special variety of the baroque called the metaphysical — will strike many English and American readers. Donne, Herbert, Crashaw, and the whole cluster of associated poets — Revius reveals that in his own unique way he is one of them.

Almost all of Revius' poetry reveals his personal involvement in the Word of God. Even the order in which he arranges his poems indicates his acknowledgment of the importance of Scripture. Since all of his sacred poems are related to Scriptural truths or situations, he arranges them in the order in which they appear in the Bible. *Book I* presents the doctrines of God, creation, and the fall, and continues with other Old Testament doctrines and history. *Book II* celebrates the birth, ministry, suffering, and death of Christ; the history of the early church; and the final judgment with its emphasis upon subsequent glory or damnation. The *Overige Gedichten* (*Remaining Poems*, so entitled by Smit), which follow the Scripturally ordered poems, reflect Revius' ardent belief that the Dutch struggles against Spanish-Catholic domination constitute the continuing battle of the militant church. In all of this Scriptural, doctrinal, and national poetry Revius is not an objective reporter but a passionate participant as a struggling but confident member of the spiritual body of Christ.

Revius fitted a wide variety of verse forms into the Scriptural order of the *Over-Ysselsche Sangen en Dichten*: sonnets which formed equally eloquent vehicles for spiritual subjects and patriotic eulogies; epigrams ranging from pert moral maxims to curt or comic criticism; song-like ballads reflecting warm devotion; modified odes with a reverent splendor; and the kind of tour de force which delights with puns and other types of word-play. Revius also included three adaptations of books from the Bible: versifications of the *Song of Solomon* and the *Lamentations of Jeremiah*; and *Haman*, a tragedy on the book of Esther. Although parts of these longer works are effective, Revius' genius is much more evident in his shorter lyrics. I have limited my translations, therefore, to representative examples of the shorter poems. These translations appear here in the Scriptural order which Revius prescribed. There are many gaps, of course, since I have selected only sixty-five of the approximately five hundred poems in the original volumes. While maintaining the original order, these selections reveal also the great variety of Revius' poetry. For here is a poet who begins with the resonant splendor of creation (p. 39); makes both wry and rich comment on the fall (pp. 49 and 51); exercises his verbal ingenuity in poems on the flood and on the Reformation (pp. 57, 127, 129, and 149); celebrates both the death of Christ and the death of Casimir in a universal context (pp. 87 and 153); and finally addresses his critics with an almost "snippy tongue" (p. 173). Such a poet cannot be called a "narrow Calvinist" but rather a great Christian who unites the mysteries of heaven with the realism of earth in the metaphors of his poetry.

Revius' poetry — its meaning through its metaphor — that is the subject of the following section of this introduction. My chief purpose is to explicate the poetry. All references to and comparisons with English metaphysical poetry are introduced chiefly to illuminate the reading of the Revius poems, through both comparison and contrast. I acknowledge with gratitude the profound and pertinent contributions of the critics listed in my bibliography — critics so well known that all students of seventeenth-century literature will recognize my debt to them. Revius' poetry evidences much of the baroque as it is generally defined: the sensuous, passionate investigation of the paradoxical oppositions displayed in the universe, and the use of all the stylistic devices which delineate these oppositions — elaborate conceits, antithesis, hyperbole, oxymoron, parallelism, and paradox. But these baroque tendencies are almost constantly informed by the metaphysical mind. This mind blends the senses and the passions with the disciplining intellect. It tensely orders and rationally argues the mysterious oppositions into a logical unity. It shows through its conceits how all apparent contradictions are finally transcended in a God-centered universe — a universe demonstrating correspondences everywhere. And in Revius it is the Protestant-Calvinist spirit, rather than the Baroque-Metaphysical, which sets the predominant tone.

THE POEMS

Revius wrote many epigrammatic poems. Although most of these cannot be called metaphysical, their concentrated wit, ingenious metaphors, and paradoxical analogies form one of the strains from which his metaphysical tendencies develop. Like that of his English contemporaries, Revius' poetry verifies Helen Gardner's comment that a metaphysical poem is something like an expanded epigram.[1] The passionate, the sensuous, and the dramatic — these metaphysical elements are usually not present in Revius' epigrams; but the ratiocination, the attempt to reconcile oppositions in a kind of conceit, and even the function of this conceit in demonstrating and illuminating an underlying metaphysical concept — these may sometimes be found. One of the basic oppositions which both Revius' Calvinistic creed and his poetry seek to resolve is that between the individual and the world around him. The sonnet "Creation" (p. 39) exemplifies richly how Revius attempts to reconcile the image of the universe as a God-glorifying lute with the disrupting element of man's perverseness.[2] Only the "learned fingers" of God can restore the harmony of perfection. The epigram "Round World" (p. 41) strives for a similar synthesis less successfully. It cleverly attempts to make man

14

an integral part of his round world by noting his failure to be straight and upright. The figure is inadequate, however, because the qualities compared are not justly related to the implied metaphysical ideals of roundness and uprightness. In "Shortest Day" and "Shortest Night" (p. 43) the witty double analogy comes nearer to the metaphysical mode. The inevitably alternating length of day and night are emphasized by the monotonous similarity of the rhythmical patterns in the two quatrains. In such a universe the brief joy and eternal suffering of sinners, and the brief sorrow and eternal joy of Christians become as natural and inevitable as the God-ordained alternation of day and night. Although still couched in the tersely logical terms of the epigram, the relationship of man to his universe and of nature to grace is the same as that which comes to more passionate expression in the sestet of "Murder of the Innocents" (p. 85): its "hasty step through death to life and rest"; its emphasis on the extreme brevity of the time of tears and the corresponding increase of eternal joy; and its additional paradox that they who lose their temporary mothers are instantly embraced by their eternal Father. As in this sonnet, so also in some of Revius' epigrams, the wit one expects to find is so tempered by emotion that it approaches the "blend of passion and thought" that T. S. Eliot associates with metaphysical poetry. With Herbert-like simplicity and devotion "Short Prayer" (p. 123) expresses the extremes of human perverseness and divine providence and the faith that paradoxically recognizes an answer in unanswered prayer. And in the awed exclamations and rhetorical questions of the two epigrams on the "Death of Christ" (p. 119) one senses not only the rational exploitation of the paradox that a divine death was needed to make death die, but also something of the triumph with which John Donne exclaims, "Death thou shalt die" and of the awe with which he says in another poem,

Who sees Gods face, that is selfe life, must dye;
What a death were it then to see God dye?
(Good Friday, 1613. Riding Westward)

Even in his epigrams, then, Revius begins to blend the expected thought with the unexpected passion in the Calvinistic but highly personal expression of his faith.

Essential to Revius' Calvinism is the synthesis of the physical and the spiritual — the worlds of nature and of grace. The all-embracing metaphor by which he achieves this synthesis is the image of the Christ, in whom God, man, and all things are finally reconciled, so that God may be in all (Cf. Ephesians 1:10 and I Corinthians 15:28). In his lyrics this is the theological base — enriched constantly by mystery and love — which his images illuminate and upon which they function. "Suffering of Christ" (p. 101) begins with the miracle of bringing forth the round creation from nothing.[3] The second quatrain proceeds to the far greater miracle of reconciling the spotless perfection of heaven with the filth of sinners, and the debts of man with the debtless wealth of Christ. In the sestet, both stony rocks and human hearts stand in awe of the miracle of redemption. The moving devotion of the last lines, in which Revius contemplates the incomprehensible suffering of Christ, is like that which Herbert expresses in "The Agonie":

Who knows not Love, let him assay
And taste that juice, which on the crosse a pike
Did set again abroach; then let him say
If ever he did taste the like . . . .

And the merging of the miracle of creation from nothing with the greater miracle of redemption recalls these lines from Crashaw:

The world was made of *Nothing* then;
'Tis made by *Nothing* now againe.
(*And he answered them nothing*)

16

The ritual symbols of "The Lord's Supper" (p. 103) function in a similar way. The sonnet abounds in baroque imagery — the sensuous elements of food and drink; the merging of Old and New Testament figures into food for the poet's soul; the feeding of both the dead and the living with the same spiritual food; the filling of both heart and mouth with sweet praise; and the up-and-down movement which connects heaven and earth, God's high hand and man's aspiring soul. The sonnet's closing line — "His blood is truly wine, his flesh is truly meat" — may seem unusual for a Calvinist theologian, but in reality it reflects Calvin's metonymical interpretation of the sacrament as well as the idea of correspondences typical of metaphysical poetry.[4]

The red-specked landscape of "Bloody Sweat" (p. 107) also embodies many of the baroque, "Crashavian" aspects of English metaphysical poetry. The ecstatic expression of religious experience through sensuous imagery; the irregular ode form; the mystical contemplation of Christ's suffering; the macabre vision of the white flowers reddened by Christ's holy blood; the almost surrealistic springing up of the flower of God's grace — all of these are reminiscent of Crashaw. The dew on the primroses and lilies merges with Magdalene's tears in Crashaw's "The Weeper" as the redness of the carnations and tulips merges with the blood of Christ in Revius' "Bloody Sweat." But the smaller compass, the greater restraint, the intensely personal colloquy of the poet with his own soul, and the meaningful relationship to the underlying theological doctrine all reflect the influence of Revius' Dutch Calvinism. As the blood of Christ transforms not only the soul of the sinner but even the flowers of the garden, it symbolizes not only the redemption of man but also the redemption of the whole universe. The Calvinist ideal of bringing all things into subjection to God restrains and directs the ecstatic devotion of the poet's

17

heart as it captures the cosmic significance of the suffering of Christ.[5]

The synthesis of nature and grace in a cosmic image is even more evident in "Circumcision" (p. 87). To regard the blood of the circumcision as prophetic of the blood of the crucifixion is not uncommon to baroque poets. Crashaw uses such a figure in "Our Lord in his Circumcision to his Father." Revius, however, adds a significant dimension to the comparison when he combines the circumcision-crucifixion theme with that of the red of sunrise and sunset. In each metaphor the worlds of creation and redemption merge: the portentous red of sunrise with the prophetic red of Christ's circumcision; the stormy crimson of sunset with Christ's "red" death on the cross; and the prediction of a serene dawn with the promise of heaven's eternal day. The sensuous color, swirling rhythm, and ecstatic vision common to the baroque all serve to illuminate the underlying theological concept of a cosmic redemption. In the manner of an El Greco *Crucifixion* the figure of the bleeding Christ is seen against the stormy heavens. Through his birth and death the sunrise and sunset of each day gain eternal significance. And through the blood and pain of the same birth and death shines the sun of God's grace, by which the suffering of sinners is forever dissolved.

Together with its tendency to reconcile oppositions and to illuminate underlying theological concepts, metaphysical poetry is usually highly personal. Although — as Frank Warnke indicates in his comments on Revius[6] — the moralizing, Scripturally oriented preacher in Revius is often evident, the element of personal devotion is certainly not absent from his poetry. In some of his best lyrics this intensely personal tone causes the Scriptural past to merge in a remarkable way with the historical present. Although the sonnet "Peter's Tears" (p. 111) speaks through the persona of Peter, its exclamatory style, swaying steps, eyes flowing

like rivers, and growing self-accusation are so vivid that
they become vicarious. With Herbert-like simplicity and
despair the poet (as well as Peter) asks, "What cheer have
you to give my cheerless heart?" And in the last three
lines both the ingenuity of the three-one contrast and the
overwhelming devotion of the words "Stand still just once
and see my bitter crying" are as personal as John Donne's
involvement when he says,

> . . . and thou looks't towards mee,
> O Saviour, as thou hang'st upon the tree . . . .
> (Good Friday, 1613. Riding Westward)

More overtly personal is Revius' best-known sonnet "He
Bore Our Griefs" (p. 115). With the emphasis and intimacy
of conversation Revius paradoxically denies the Jews' part
in the crucifixion, and himself becomes the cross, the whip,
the nail, and the spear which inflicted Christ's suffering.
Again the past and the present, unconscious matter and
imperfect man are brought together in the poet's personal
vision of the cross. And again like John Donne (Divine
Poems, Sonnet XII), Revius grieves that his own sins far
surpass the Jews' impiety. Similarly paradoxical and personal is "His Blood Be on Us and on Our Children"
(p. 113), even though it falls short of emotional intensity
and remains epigrammatic. The curse which becomes a
blessing is the kind of paradox in which Frank Warnke sees
the metaphysical poet's attempt to clarify theological mysteries.[7] The witty antitheses touch on various Calvinist
dogmas: the incomprehensible irony by which the same
blood can both save and condemn; the incomprehensible
grace by which sin becomes salvation for the saint; and
the incomprehensible manner in which hard-hearted rejec-
tion and humble repentance are both "free" in spite of the
indubitable sovereignty of God.

Many more of Revius' poems reveal intense personal involvement in the illuminating of theological mysteries. Sometimes, as in "Burning Bush" (p. 59), the individual functions as member of the body of Christ. For Revius, however, this relationship was experienced as well as revealed. Although the miracle of the burning bush vitalizes especially the doctrine of God's providential care of his church, the shepherd Moses and the poet Revius give it personal immediacy. Also the many poems which probe the paradoxes of Scripture reveal that Revius is personally involved as well as intellectually intrigued. In the sonnet "Mary" (p. 77) the paradox of the incarnation informs the whole poem, as it does in the second sonnet of Donne's *La Corona*, where Donne speaks to Mary of the Christ:

> . . . [He] is thy Sonne, and Brother;
> Whom thou conceiv'st, conceiv'd; yea thou art now
> Thy Makers maker, and thy Fathers mother . . . .

The translation of Revius' sonnet reveals that he particularizes the paradox in a similar way:

> Most blessed she, the sister of her child,
> Daughter of Him whom she herself gave birth,
> The bride of Him who from her womb came forth . . . .

The last three lines of the sonnet evidence Revius' personal — and naturally Protestant — involvement as he reveals that the supreme blessedness, both for Mary and for all Christians, lies in being spiritually, not physically, united with the Christ.

The poem "Nativity" (p. 79) is similarly paradoxical and personal, but in a quite different tone. The rhythmical ballad stanzas, continual internal rhymes, diminutives, and tender attitude all combine to set the mood of a song-like lullaby. Yet in each simple stanza appears a startling paradox, creating an unusual sense of incongruity — the same kind of gracious incongruity that invests with divinity the tiny baby lying in the manger. Personal devotion illuminates the poet's adoration of the holy child. The quaint paradoxes are delightfully related to the homely manger scene, yet simultaneously illustrative of the incomprehensible mystery which it embraces. The "orphaned" Christ and the "adopted" children; the dirty stall and the clean heavens; the cold wind and the warm love — these and all of the other paradoxes find a moving climax in the last stanza, where the poet prays that the wee infant be born also in him. The whole poem — reminiscent of Herbert in its devotional simplicity and of Donne in its functioning through paradox — is given an inimitable Revius quality by its many feminine rhymes and its homely Dutch tone. Much of this quality — sad to say — my translation fails to capture, but hopefully it will be able at least to suggest the spirit of the poem. Perhaps it will also reveal that Revius is here inspired by the same spirit of awe that moved Crashaw to write his well-known lines:

Welcome, all *wonders* in one sight!
  Eternitie shut in a span,
Summer in winter, day in night,
  Heaven in Earth, and God in man;
Great little one! whose all embracing birth
Lifts earth to heav'n, stoops heav'n to earth.
           (An Hymne of the Nativity . . .)

In "Sinful Woman" (p. 97) Revius treats the common baroque motif of the tears and adoration of Mary Magdalene. Her eyes become a basin for Christ's feet; her hair a towel to dry his ankles; and her neck his footstool. Although some of the conceits are reminiscent of the sensuous extremes of Crashaw's "The Weeper," Revius' emphasis is not on the tears or on Magdalene herself, but rather on the divine love of Christ. This emphasis — perhaps too heavily moralistic — is given a meaningful dimension by relating it to the electing love of God, which is the sole source of Magdalene's love. As the latter stanzas stress the source of each of Magdalene's acts in the purifying look, cleansing blood, and spiritual kiss of her Savior, one senses the theological note of divine election which functions through the conceits. And although the last stanza sounds too much like a closing moral, it is certainly Revius' personal faith that sets himself with Magdalene among those who show gratitude only because they are saved by grace:

> Our failures are all covered by his merit
> That we may never cease his will to do.

Like most metaphysical poets Revius uses few images from classical mythology. When he does use them, they function in the manner of the conceit, bringing together the apparent contradictions of heathen myth and Christian revelation. Beneath these images lies the Calvinist preacher's attempt to bring the rich world of renaissance humanism into proper subjection to God and to full fruition in Him. The poem "Law Gives Knowledge of Sin" (p. 61) stresses the opposition between man-centered humanism and God-centered Calvinism: Narcissus, melting away in tears of insatiable self-love, is contrasted with the poet's soul, losing itself in tears of complete self-abnegation. In the sonnet "Praise of Jesus Christ" (p. 75),[8] however, the use of and contrasts with mythological figures function much more richly. The painful thirsting after poetic inspiration from mythological sources is recognized in and yet transcended by the poet's sweeter, nobler aspirations. Ingeniously Phoebus is replaced by the Sun (or Son), the laurel wreath by the twisted thorns, and Pegasus by the Spirit-Dove. The entire sonnet is informed by a fervor in which poetic inspiration and religious devotion merge. The rich but inadequate figures of mythology may die out, but

both the Christ and the song he inspires will endure forever. What Abraham Cowley says in his poem "On the
Death of Mr. Crashaw" is also true of Revius: he attempts
to bring the muses "home back to their *Holy Land*."

This use of classical myth occurs also in one of the poems
of Revius' last important genre: the patriotic and laudatory
sonnets of the poems which Professor Smit has entitled
Overige Gedichten (pp. 131–73). In "Elegy" (p. 153) the
mythical boat crossing the Styx becomes Elijah's chariot,
sweeping toward heaven. As Abraham Cowley sees the
Christian poet Crashaw "mount *Alive* the skies . . . ," so
here Revius sees the Christian patriot Casimir climbing
home to God. "Elegy" (p. 155) begins with the paradoxes
of cold heat, shivering sweat, talking tongues turned dumb,
and sweetness turned bitter. But in the sestet the rich earth
welcomes Casimir's discarded mold, and the glowing
heavens beg for the added glory of his soul, which now
appears as a star. One senses here the poet's attempt to
invest the sad death of the hero of God's people with
cosmic splendor and to envision his influential planet as
an inspiration for the heroes of the future. In the following
"Elegy" (p. 157) the tears of Friesland's people become
more than mere baroque decorations: they join the angry
elements of nature in swearing a vengeance that springs up
suddenly from the powerful source of unexpected and overwhelming grief. In "Prince's Praise" (p. 159) both the sen-
timent of the poem and the cleverly executed figure of the
prince cutting his own immortal statue are reminiscent of
Milton's tribute to Shakespeare. Although addressed to the
Netherlands rather than to the dead hero, Revius' words
suggest Milton's lines:

> Thou in our wonder and astonishment
> Hast built thy self a live-long Monument.
> > (On Shakespear. 1630)

In some of the other sonnets of this group, the Biblical overtones makes Revius' attempt to merge the Scriptural past with his own contemporary situation more overt. In "War" (p. 161) the horrors of battle, the reverence of prayer, and the hope for peace are all brought together in an atmosphere suggestive of Old Testament incense and the prayers of Samuel for military victory (Cf. I Samuel 7:5–10). In "Flood of Tears" (p. 167) — even though its images are somewhat contradictory — the small cloud and rising floods suggest the account of Elijah's victorious contest with the prophets of Baal (I Kings 18). In "Thankfulness" (p. 169) Revius brings this tendency to merge the republic of the Protestant Netherlands with the universal image of the kingdom of God to a delightful climax. The homely intimacy of the candle-lit towns and villages and their reflection of the starlit heavens seem to bring Holland and heaven very close together; the warm affection for the Prince and the fond pride that dares to compare Holland with heaven seem to validate the implication that Prince Frederick Henry could naturally be a citizen of both. In using such ingenious devices to bring together heaven and earth, the Biblical past and the historical present, the lasting battle of the militant church and the temporal struggles of the Dutch Protestants, Revius is stressing the kind of universal correspondences which Mazzeo associates with metaphysical poetry (see note 1).

I do not present this explication of the translations in this volume as definitive or complete. I have explicated the poems in groups (not necessarily mutually exclusive) which demonstrate certain of Revius' metaphysical tendencies. This has naturally — and desirably — left some of the translations standing without comment. But the reader will probably note their relationship to the various characteristics I have discussed: the epigrammatic wit and moralizing; the simultaneous relationship to the Bible and to the poet's personal experience; the delight in conceit and in various ingenious devices; the rising to a lyric climax in the poems on the Christ; the militant Calvinist-Protestantism; and the fervent patriotism. In comparing Revius with his English contemporaries, my chief purpose has not been to prove that Revius is a metaphysical poet but rather to aid in the interpretation of his significant and beautiful poems. For my explication stresses one man's poetic probing of the mysterious contradictions of existence and of their final reconciliation in God. And, whatever the manner, that is the matter of which great poetry can be made.

THE TRANSLATIONS

The attempt to translate poetry is a mixture of pleasure and pain. The pleasure, I believe, must come at the beginning and end of the process, and the pain must lie hidden between. Some readers — particularly those interested in the art of translation — may welcome a partial analysis of the painstaking intricacies of the translator's task. It is for them especially that I include this section of my introduction. Hopefully, it may increase the pleasure of reading the translated poem. Translated poem, I say, for therein lies the rub. The translation must itself be a poem. If it is not, the translator's pains have been only pathetic and pedantic, and the translation becomes a mere parody.

For me the basic requirement of achieving a poem and not a parody established an initial prohibition, which I have observed throughout: the translator must not begin by writing a prose translation. In other words, each translation must begin in pleasure and inspiration, not in pedantry and transliteration. For each of my attempts this has been true. Regardless of what effect the finished translation may have on the reader, for me it has always begun

in pleasure — the pleasure of discovering the genius of a
Revius poem; of letting that poem become a part of my-
self; of sensing one of its phrases, lines, or stanzas coming
to life in the English language; of coaxing and nurturing
this core — under the disciplining direction of the original — to expand into a poem that would *be* in the English
what the Revius poem is in the Dutch. For me this is the
only way for a translation, at least the translation of a short
lyric, to begin. Robert Frost once said that a poem may
be worked after it is in existence, but that it may never be
worked into existence.[9] So also of a translation. It must
be initially inspired, even though that inspiration is not a
Pegasus, a Parnassus, or even a personal experience, but
rather a poem.

Constantly accompanying and informing my basic prin-
ciple — that the translation must itself be a poem — were
two other inevitable working principles: the translated
poem must convey as precisely as possible the meaning and
tone of the original; and this meaning and tone must be
caught in a form as similar as possible to the original. These
exacting demands for authentic reading and precise render-
ing were naturally present from the start. But after a first
draft had developed, the more arduous and painstaking
application of these principles began. The poeticisms, in-
versions, and archaisms which appear in Revius' poems
complicated these demands. Dutch readers will note that
Revius' language includes many seventeenth-century pecu-
liarities: *doe* for *toen*; *en . . . niet* for *niet*; *haer* for *hun*;
na for *naar*; *wt for uit*; and various others. I found, however, that I could achieve a natural translation only through
using twentieth-century diction. To catch the authentic
meaning in spite of this modernizing of diction, it was
helpful at this point to write a literal prose translation of
each poem. This prose translation, with all its pungent awk-
wardness set next to my first draft, played the part of an

extremely demanding, practical, and penetrating critic. Sometimes its suggestions seemed suddenly obvious: of course, "Mild heaven-dew" is better for *O milden hemels-dou* than "O heavenly dew" (The Lord's Supper, p. 103, l. 7). Sometimes it caused days of vacillating, consulting dictionaries, and sounding out friends: Should *reyne salen* be translated "clean salons" or "spotless halls" (Suffering of Christ, p. 101, l. 6)? Sometimes it forced such shattering changes that I had to rewrite whole stanzas, whole sections, or even whole poems. I still feel regret for many lost lines, which, like the following, were the results of misreading the original:

> The heavens, long preparing for this day,
>   Beg you to come to multiply their glow
> And promise none but heroes shall be born
> Under this star, that took our Prince away.
>   (Cf. Elegy, p. 155, ll. 11-14)

And sometimes the lost lines became lost poems because the unique word-plays, puns, or paradoxes proved impossible to convey in an English poem.

In addition to adjusting my first draft to the demands of the literal translation came the equally rigorous exercise of comparing each element of the poetic form — the prosody involved. Compromise, approximation, substitution — all these were part of the intriguing process. The general form of the original I wished always to preserve: the sonnet, the epigram, the ballad-like quatrain, the loose ode form. Most of Revius' sonnets — usually written in the French-inspired alexandrine line — developed much more naturally for me in the pentameter line to which the English ear has become attuned. Of the twenty-one sonnets I have translated, only four of the originals had been written in the pentameter (pp. 83, 101, 111, 151). All of my translations began as pentameters, but three of them demanded a change to the heavier hexameter: "Fall" (p. 51), partly because of the somber doom it pronounces on the serpent and partly because of its repeated accusing exclamations; "Elegy" (p. 153), because of the underworld atmosphere of its octave, which lost its oppressive weight in the pentameter form; and "Flood of Tears" (p. 165), because of the military clamor involved and the indispensable antithesis of the last line. In two others I took the freedom of lengthening only the closing line into a hexameter: "The Lord's Supper" (p. 103) and "Flood of Tears" (p. 167), in both cases to strengthen the balance and conclusiveness of the ending. In all of the sonnets I changed the *abba abba* rhyme scheme of Revius' French octave to *abba cddc*; I then proceeded with variations of the rhyme of his sestet. In the sonnets, as in the other poems, I replaced perfect rhyme with near rhyme or even unrhymed words when necessary (e.g. Creation, p. 39, ll. 1 and 4; 5 and 8; 9 and 10). In all of these deliberations and decisions I attempted both to recognize and to transcend the differences between Revius' sonnet form and my own anglicized version of it.

The other verse forms demanded other adjustments. In the epigrams and epitaphs I considered it most important to retain the precise, balanced form and the point or punch line of each poem. This necessitated and, in my opinion, allowed some freedom in manipulating the subsidiary ideas involved. In "Round World" (p. 41), e.g., I added the word *man* to attain rhyme and balance, even though the original presents only the abstract quality of man's uprightness. In "Burning Bush" (p. 59) the form itself required adjustment. I had to substitute near rhyme for perfect rhyme in order to preserve other formal elements: alternate pairs of feminine and masculine endings, parallel syntax in corresponding lines of the two quatrains, repetition of the key word *Lord*, and the long-drawn-out emphasis on the last two words: *preserving evermore* for *laetse nimmermeer*.

In ". . . Canonization . . ." (p. 149) I shortened the poem because the two extra lines seemed to detract from the effectiveness of the pun in English. This poem demonstrates also my practice of abiding by Revius' indention, even though the logic by which he usually proceeds (indenting the masculine lines and not the feminine) is often lost in my translations.

With three of Revius' finest poems — "Nativity" (p. 79), "Circumcision" (p. 87), and "Bloody Sweat" (p. 107) — my decision to preserve the extremely intricate verse forms forced me to translate the texts very freely. I regret the substitutions, approximations, and compromises which sometimes resulted. In "Nativity" (p. 79) the demands of the original were overwhelming: end rhyme, internal rhyme, simple language, and the preservation of the central paradox in each stanza. I have earnestly attempted to make the translation convey something of the folk-like simplicity, devotional dignity, and doctrinal mystery of the original; something of the almost playful yet always tender piling up of the paradoxes that attend the humble birth of the Creator-King.

In "Circumcision" (p. 87) the difficulties seemed almost insurmountable. The uneven line-lengths; the stormy, hesitant rhythms; the premonitory pauses; the climactic development of each stanza; the mesmeric repetitions of feminine endings and double and triple rhymes — all of these were necessary to convey initially the somber significance and finally the brilliant triumph of the original. Revius formed many of his feminine rhymes by using finite verbs and plural nouns ending in *en*; I tried to create a similar effect by using many participles (*revealing, stealing, appealing, concealing* in stanza one) and several *ion* nouns (*decision, precision, vision, circumcision* in stanza two). Comparing the translation with the original will reveal other measures I have used in my attempt to capture the dignity, color, and grandeur of "Circumcision." I hope

29

that even a partially unsuccessful attempt will suggest the unique splendor of this great ode.

And so also in "Bloody Sweat" (p. 107). Using substitute-words of similar tonal effect (*Gethsemane* for *Oliveten* in stanza one); adapting and switching the position of adjectives (*tearing*, *bursting*, and *thousand-thousand* in stanza two); trying to weave corresponding patterns of alliteration (*Creator*, *creeps*, and *crimson* to balance the *Siet*, *Schepper*, and *sonden* of the original in stanza two) — these are some of the means by which I tried to convey the oddly hesitant and often catalectic trochees of the original rhythms and the poignant music of the Dutch words and phrases. Again, the translation may give only a hint of the sensuous richness of the original. But getting a hint of the greatness of a poem is better than not reading it at all.

And so continued the detailed process of revision: adapting, adjusting, polishing, perfecting. Sometimes, fortuitously, the most literal translations afforded also the most nearly corresponding patterns:

De Heer ons Vader is, de aerde onse moeder . . .
The Lord our Father is, the earth our mother . . .
(Pp. 44 and 45)

In the epigrammatic poems this occurred more than in the sonnets and other lyrics. In "Shortest Day" and "Shortest Night" such corresponding patterns developed:

Den cortsten dach de langste nacht.
The shortest day the longest night.
(p. 43)

But even these short quatrains demanded several adjustments. A necessary shift in the position of a word may rob it of a desirable emphasis:

. . . maer t' bitter truyren . . .
. . . your woe will be . . .

The word *woe*, especially where it stands in the line, cannot convey the pain of the longer word *truyren*, especially in its position at the end of the line. The reversal which became necessary in the last line of "Cortste Nacht" seemed less damaging than the *truyren-woe* exchange since it still allowed a four-syllable word with a final, open-vowel sound to end the line:

Maer eeuwichlijck sult ghy verblijden.
You will rejoice eternally.

However, in spite of my attempts in these two quatrains to use shorter words — as Revius seems to do — for the "time" ideas and longer words for the "eternity" ideas, the translations still fail to convey the full effect of the originals.

In the sonnets — partly because of the change from hexameter to pentameter lines — parallel patterns of syntax, alliteration, and assonance developed very rarely. Sometimes, however, the naturally emerging sound patterns of the translation, although differing from the original, did finally stress similar sequences of significant words:

Gesegent is de maecht de croon van alle maechden,
Den tempel van Gods Soon en wesentlijcke cracht,
Den schonen dageraet waer door ons nu toe-lacht
De Sonne daer soo dick de Vaderen na vraechden.
Most blessed is this maid, all virgins' crown,
The temple of God's Son and of His might,
The dawn through which the long-awaited light
Of heaven's rising Sun comes smiling down.
                                        (Maria, pp. 76 and 77)

The additional emphasis which *maecht* (l. 1) receives from the subsequent word *maechden* is lost in the *maid-virgins'* sequence of the translation. I hope, however, that the *Most-maid-temple-might* pattern of the translation (ll. 1–2) produces a similar effect. Although the alliterative connection

31

between *croon* and *cracht* (ll. 1–2) is lost in the translation, I hope that rhyming it with *down* gives a comparable intensity to *crown*. Similarly, the subtle assonance of *Gesegent* and *wesentlijcke*, lost in the translation of lines one and two, is at least partially redeemed by the assonance of *blessed* and *temple*. In the sonnets it was rarely possible to strike a translation like the following — a line in which the syntax, the alliteration, and even some of the assonance of the original repeat themselves naturally in the translation:

> En tooch den lauwer-hoet van haren blonden hare.
> And tore the laurel hat from her blond hair.
>
> (Elegy, pp. 156 and 157, l. 8)

Even such similarity to the original, of course, was no guarantee of having attained the best possible translation.

Many other difficult choices — euphemistically called translator's freedoms — were forced upon me. In the case of Revius' numerous feminine rhymes, my decisions varied according to the number of suitable trochaic words available in English. In "Body and Soul" (p. 45), "Satan and Eve" (p. 49), and several others the feminine endings were easy to preserve; in such long lyrics as "Circumcision" (p. 87) and "Sinful Woman" (p. 97) — where I felt they had to be preserved — the sonorous quality I wished to obtain may sound too pompous (p. 87) and the gentle too sentimental (p. 97). In other poems I preserved feminine endings only by making concessions: the sight-rhyme of *fingers* with *singers* in "Creation" (p. 39, ll. 9–10), or the shifting into an unusual rhyme scheme in the sestet of "Peter's Tears" (p. 111). In still others I tried to simulate feminine endings by using words ending with sybillant or liquid consonants instead (cf. Elegy, p. 155, ll. 13–14; and Fall, p. 14, l. 4).

Having noted, then, the initial surge of pleasure with which a translation begins and the painstaking process by which it develops toward its final form, I hope that the reader may find the final pleasure for which the translations exist: discovering some of the delight of reading Revius' poems. I hope that my translations have preserved their pulsating life. For, as Paul Engle has said,

> Once upon a time, translation meant the direct removal of an earthly soul to heaven, without an intervening death.
>
> Too often, in the translation of a poem from one language to another, the text suffers an actual death.[10]

If through my work Revius' poems have not suffered a death but rather risen to new life, the long process was well worthwhile. For then, even though the fiery chariot of translation sometimes jolted and jarred painfully, the poems have finally arrived to live again in a new land and in a new language.

NOTES *to the Introduction*

[1] Helen Gardner, "Introduction," *The Metaphysical Poets* (Baltimore, 1957), p. 18. For a somewhat opposing view see Joseph Anthony Mazzeo, "A Critique of Some Modern Theories of Metaphysical Poetry," *Modern Philology*, L (November, 1952), p. 91.

[2] Cf. J. C. Arens, "Twee Sonnetten bij Revius en Drummond," *Neophilologus*, 47(1963), 151–153. Arens indicates the great similarity between this Revius sonnet and the sonnet "On the Book" by William Drummond of Hawthornden and a possible source for both in a French sonnet by Simon Goulart (1543–1606).

[3] Cf. Arens, pp. 151–152. This is the second of the pair of sonnets in which Arens indicates connections between Revius and Drummond (in the sonnet entitled "Amazement at the Incarnation of God"). See the annotation in my bibliography for a further description of Arens' work on Revius' sources.

[4] See Calvin's *Institutes*, Book IV, Chapter 17, Section 21, and the article by Mazzeo cited in note 1.

[5] This cosmic significance of Christ's redemptive work is clearly reflected in John Calvin's *Commentaries*, especially in his explications of I Corinthians 27 and Romans 8. Of I Corinthians 27:27 Calvin says, "For the earth was *cursed* . . . and everything that it contains; and it is through Christ alone that we recover what has been taken from us." Of verse 28 he says, ". . . all things will be brought back to God . . . that they may be closely bound to him." On Romans 8:19 Calvin says, "There is no element and no part of the world which, touched with the knowledge of its present misery, is not intent on the hope of the resurrection." This doctrine by no means contradicts Calvin's interpretation of election but rather complements it. His exegesis of Romans 8:21 states clearly that "all innocent creatures from earth to heaven

34

are punished for our sins." When the sons of God are restored to the "excellence of glory . . . all creatures shall be renewed . . . [and] God will restore the present fallen world to perfect condition. . . ." In Calvin's view not only "the elect" but also the whole unconscious universe, which now "groaneth and travaileth" (Romans 8:22), will one day be glorified through Christ's redeeming work.

[6] Frank J. Warnke, *European Metaphysical Poetry* (New Haven and London, 1961), p. 66.

[7] Warnke, p. 7 and pp. 67–68.

[8] Cf. J. C. Arens, "Mijn Dobbele Parnas: Revius en Du Bartas," *De Nieuwe Taalgids*, 56(1963), 58. Arens here indicates connections between Revius and Du Bartas and a slight similarity between this Revius sonnet and Drummond's sonnet "Nature Must Yield to Grace."

[9] Robert Frost, *Complete Poems of Robert Frost* (New York, 1949), p. viii.

[10] Paul Engle, "Postface," *Contemporary French Poetry*, ed. Alexander Aspel and Donald Justice (Ann Arbor, 1965), p. 190.

OLD TESTAMENT POEMS

EERSTE BOECK

SCHEPPINGE

God heeft de werelt door onsichtbare clavieren
Betrocken als een luyt met al sijn toebehoor.
Den hemel is de bocht vol reyen door en door,
Het roosken, son en maen die om ons hene swieren.

   Twee grove bassen die staech bulderen en tieren
Sijn d'aerd en d'oceaan: de quinte die het oor
Verheuget, is de locht: de reste die den choor
Volmaket, is t'geboomt en allerhande dieren.

   Dees luyte sloech de Heer met sijn geleerde vingers,
De engels stemden in als treffelicke singers,
De bergen hoorden toe, de vloeden stonden stil:

   Den mensch alleen en hoort noch sangeren noch snaren,
Behalven dien't de Heer belieft te openbaren
Na sijn bescheyden raet en Goddelijcken wil.

CREATION

The world is like a lute which God has strung
With strings invisible; the heavens around
Make up the ridged and arching board of sound,
The music-hole, the rhythmic moon and sun.
    The surging ocean and the moaning earth
Are giant basses both; the gentle breeze
Makes up the higher strings; the moving trees
And animals fill out the middle choir.
    This lute the Master struck with learnèd fingers,
The angels formed a band of skillful singers,
The mountains leaned to listen, floods stood still;
    But man alone hears neither strings nor voice
Unless the sovereign Lord makes him his choice
By his determined counsel and his will.

WERELT RONT

Het rond' is nimmer recht, het ronde draeyt ront-om,
En watmen daer aen siet gebogen is en crom:
Ist wonder dattet noch by onse tijt gebeuret
Dat in des werelts rond' geen recht en wort gespeuret?

ROUND WORLD

The round is never straight, a round thing turns around,
And in it only bent and crooked parts are found.
Is it a wonder then that in this round earth's span
There never has been found a straight and upright man?

CORTSTEN DACH

Den cortsten dach de langste nacht.
O sondaer neemt doch hier op acht:
U vreucht is cort, maer t'bitter truyren
Dat daer op volgt sal eeuwich duyren.

CORTSTE NACHT

De cortste nacht den langsten dach.
O vrome mindert u geclach:
Cleyn is alhier en cort u lijden,
Maer eeuwichlijck sult ghy verblijden

Shortest day

The shortest day, the longest night.
O sinner, contemplate your plight:
Your joy is short, your woe will be
Prolonged through all eternity.

Shortest night

The shortest night, the longest day.
O Christian, wipe your tears away:
Though slight and short your grief will be,
You will rejoice eternally.

Lijf ende siele

De Heer ons Vader is, de aerde onse moeder,
De een het leven gaf, de ander draecht het voeder.
   Hoe comet dat den mensch van God geen werck en heeft,
   En met sijn sinlicheyt heel aende aerde cleeft?
Eylaes, het gaet so toe: de kinders allegader
Beminnen doch veel meer de moeder als den vader.

BODY AND SOUL

The Lord our Father is, the earth our mother;
The one gives life to us, our food the other.
  Why is it that all men ignore their God
  While their desires cling wholly to the sod?
Alas, but so it goes: the children bother
Much more about the mother than the father.

Man ende wijf

De mane vande son haer claricheyt genietet,
Maer t'edel sonne-licht niet vande maen en vlietet.
  De vrou treckt vanden man den naem en het geslacht,
  Maer noyt heeft dit de vrou den manne toegebracht.

T'selve

Den man sijn echte wijf alleene moet beminnen,
De vrouwe onder hem moet buygen hare sinnen.
  T'en gaet niet qualijck toe daert soo gehouden wert:
  Den man is doch het hooft, de vrouwe is het hert.

Man and wife

Although the moon reflects the sun's rays every night,
It does not, in return, give to the sun its light.
  Woman receives from man his family and name
  But never, in return, has given him the same.

The same

The man must show his wife his love in every way;
The woman must be glad his wishes to obey.
  Things will not go amiss if each fulfills his part:
  For man is still the head, and woman is the heart.

SLANGE ENDE EVA

Van Eva en de slang' het giftich tsamenspreken
De sonde heeft gebroedt en allerley gebreken.
   Hier door is in het quaet verworren onsen geest.
   Och, had de slange stom, of Eva doof geweest!

SATAN AND EVE

When Eve and Satan joined in conversation,
Sin was conceived for every man and nation.
  For all poor sinners how much better if
  The serpent had been dumb or Eve been deaf!

VAL

Wat blintheyt onbesuyst! dat Eva die God diende
Int salich paradijs, wt weelde, sonder noot
Der hellen roffiaen het ledich oore boot
En om te worden cloeck des Heeren vloeck verdiende!
    Wat wederhoricheyt! dat Adam, niet ontsiende
Noch tijdelijcke last, noch eyndelose noot,
Socht, opgeblasen puyst, te worden even groot
Als God die hem bewaerd' en dien hy had' te vriende!
    Wat duyvelscher bedroch! ghy moorder ghy verrae'r
Hebt smeeckende vervoert de kinders met de vae'r.
Wat voordeel meendy dies, o vyant, op te steken?
    Wy liggen int verderf, doch hopen op genae,
Maer uwen boosen raet brengt u de meeste schae:
Der vrouwe heylich saet sal u den cop verbreken.

FALL

What blind stupidity! That Eve in paradise
Who served the Lord in joyful luxury, not fear,
Should lend the hellish ruffian her empty ear
And thus become accursed of God instead of wise!

   What great perversity! That Adam, not afraid
Of temporary pain or any cruel fate,
Sought, like a bursting boil, to grow to be as great
As God, who was his stay and whom he had as friend!

   What diabolic fraud! You murderer, you plotter
Have cunningly misled the children with their father.
What profit could you gain, o foe, by this deceit?

   Although we lie in sin, our hope is in the cross,
But your malicious plan brings you the greatest loss!
Eve's holy seed shall crush your head beneath his feet.

ONTSCHULDINGE

Den man verclaeght het wijf, het wijf de slange wroeget,
En geen van alle dry den richter vergenoeget
   Maer yder vonnis crycht en straffe na zijn sond':
Gelijck drie swemmers, die, beginnende te sincken
D'een d'ander grijpen aen wt vrese van verdrincken
   En trecken alle dry malcander inden gront.

EXCUSES

The man accused his wife, the wife accused the snake,
And not one of the three a good excuse could make,
    But each was judged and doomed according to his sin:
Just like three swimmers who, beginning to go down,
Grasp at each other's limbs because they fear to drown
    And, struggling to get out, they pull each other in.

LEVEN

Dit leven is een vrye merckt.
Let op u stuck, en daer op merckt
Dat ghy den tijt niet laet verlopen
Gestelt tot copen en vercopen.
Want sitty stil, of blijfdy wt
Tot dat de doot de cramen sluyt,
Soo ist te laet om te beginnen
Het alderbeste goet te winnen.

LIFE

This life is like an open mart.
Wake up and get an early start!
Don't let the time go running by
Which you should use to sell and buy.
If you sit still or don't show up
Until death comes to close the shop,
Beginning then will not suffice
To gain the pearl of greatest price.

Sontvloet:
MONOSYLLABICUM

Hooch en lanck,
Breet van ganck,
Dick en starck
Was de Arck.
Daer in clam
Sem en Ham
Met zijn broer,
Vaer en moer,
En noch dry
Wijfs daer by.
Al het vee
Had daer stee.
Hart en hind,
Brack en wind',
Beyr en leeu,
Roeck en spreeu,
Peirt en os,
Haes en vos,
Swijn en aep,
Geyt en schaep,
Losch en das
Daer oock was.

Hen en haen
Specht en craen,
Duyf en paeu,
Uyl en caeu,
Raef en gier
Vant men hier.
Craey en snip
Vlooch int schip.
Musch en vinck
Daer in ginck.
Draeck en slang'
Men hier dwang'.
Hont en cat,
Muys en rat,
Groot en cleyn,
Vuyl en reyn,
Quaet en goet,
Fel en soet,
Wilt en tam
Daer toe quam.

Al wat vloog'
In het droog',
Al wat croop,
Of zijn loop
Had' opt lant
Quam ter hant.
Wat men niet
In en liet
Mensch of beest
Gaf den geest
In den grond',
Om de sond'
Die het al
Bracht ten val.
    Paer by paer
Trat daer naer
Weer aent lant,
Door Gods hant
Die liet af
Van zijn straf.
Hem, de Heer,
Sy de eer!

FLOOD:
MONOSYLLABICUM

Long and high
broad and dry
big and dark
was the ark.
There in clamb
Shem and Ham
Jafe and Ma
with their pa.
Each the wife
of his life
brought in, too,
wouldn't you?
Beast and bird
heard the word:
Go in there
pair by pair.
Horse and ox
hare and fox
dove and crow
deer and doe.
Hind and hound
could be found

in the ark
with the lark.
Cock and crab
rook and rab-
bit were there
with the bear.
Ape and swine
stood in line,
duck and drake
frog and snake
calf and cow
pig and sow
dog and cat
mouse and rat.
Foul and clean
fat and lean
short and tall
large and small
wild and tame
all the same.

Those that creep
in the deep
those that fly
in the sky.
All that earth
brought to birth
came to lie
high and dry,
not by rain
to be slain.
All out-side
drowned and died.
For the sin
of all men
brought them all
to this fall.
  Then the rain
'Gan to wane
by the word
of the Lord.
To him raise
All the praise!

BRANDENDE BOS

Hoe comtet dat den bos tot aenden hemel blaecket
En door soo grooten vier tot asschen niet geraket?
    Verwondert u des niet, o Mose, lieve man,
    Want God is inden bos diese bewaren can.
Hoe comtet dat de kerck als in een oven gloeyet
Vervolget, onderdruckt, en even heerlijck bloeyet?
    Verwondert u des niet, o Christen, want de Heer
    De Heer is in zijn kerck: die laetse nimmermeer.

BURNING BUSH

How is it that the bush whose flame to heaven flashes
By such a glowing fire is not reduced to ashes?
  Be not amazed at this, O Moses, nor surprised,
  For God is in the bush, preserving it alive.
How is it that the church, as in an oven glowing,
Is troubled and oppressed and yet forever growing?
  Be not amazed at this, O Christian, for the Lord,
  The Lord is in his church, preserving evermore.

WET, GEEFT KENNIS DER SONDEN

Narcissus, soomen seyt, hem neygend' om te drincken
En siende inde bron sijn jeugdich aenschijn blincken
   Verliefde op hemself soo deerlijck, dat met een
   In schreyen hy versmolt, in suchten hy verdween:
Eylaes, mijn droeve siel het weder-spel moet dragen.
Sy had' in haer gestalt te voren een behagen,
   Maer slaende haer gesicht op Godes reyne wet
   Sy vont haer soo mismaeckt, soo lelijck, so besmet
Dat zy een af-keer heeft, ja grouwel van haer selven
En soeckt haer in een see van tranen te bedelven.

LAW GIVES
KNOWLEDGE OF SIN

Narcissus, so men say, while bending at the brook,
Admired himself so much that he began to look
  On his own youthful face with loving, doting eyes:
  To melt in his own tears, to disappear in sighs.
Alas, my sorry soul the opposite must bear:
In former times she thought that she was very fair,
  But when she turned her face to look into God's law,
  She found herself so ugly, so hateful, that she saw
Within herself the heights of horror. Now she tries
To drown herself in tears, to melt herself in sighs.

Afcomst

K'en weet niet hoemen can met redenen verbloemen
Dat luyden sonder deucht op haer geslachte roemen.
  Want isser yemant lam of sleypet hy het been
  Wat helpt hem dat sijn vaer was rustich op zijn leen?
Stinckt yemant als een groep, wat salt hem connen baten
Dat zijn grootvader roock na soete muscheliaten?
  Staet u het heele lijf tot gavel ende ploech
  Wat passet u den helm die yemant voor u droech?
T'en is geen edelman die leeft gelijck een verken,
Dewijl den adel rijst wt deuchdelijcke wercken.

LINEAGE

I cannot understand why people care to bother
To praise a no-good man who brags about his father.
  If someone who is lame and drags a crippled limb
  Has parents with good legs, what good is that to him?
And if you smell like dung, what does it help to say
Your grandfather was fragrant as roses in his day?
  If you spend all your life with pitchfork and with plough,
  The helmet of your forebears won't suit you anyhow.
You can't live like a pig and be nobility:
Good works alone create true aristocracy.

Waerheyt

Men seyt wel, en het is oock menichmael gebleken,
Dat sotten int gemeyn de waerheyt sullen spreken.
　Men seyt oock, et het is een over-oude clacht
　Dat die de waerheyt spreeckt wort voor een sot geacht.

TRUTH

Men say — and I have seen it happen since my youth —
That fools in general are apt to speak the truth.
    But men will also say — complaining, as a rule —
    That he who speaks the truth is often thought a fool.

ACHTERCLAP

De achterclap is wt de helle voortgedrongen.
Wie achterclapt die heeft den duyvel op der tongen.
  En die vermakelijck den clapper geeft gehoor
  Die heeft, al denckt hyt niet, den duyvel in het oor.
Maer diese stracx gelooft, die moet voorseker weten
Dat hem de bose geest het herte heeft beseten.

SLANDER

It surely was in hell that slander was begun;
The slanderer still has the devil on his tongue.
  And he who is persuaded easily to hear
  The slander, he must have the devil in his ear.
But he who finally believes the false report,
He certainly must have the devil in his heart.

DRY PLAGEN

Van honger, pest, en sweirt (de roeden van Gods toren)
Heeft David voor het minst de siecte wtvercoren:
    Maer ah! mijn vaderlant, hoe gatet nu met dy!
    T'comt op geen kiesen aen, hier sijnse alle dry.

THREE PLAGUES

Of famine, pest, and sword (the judgments of God's hand)
King David chose the pest as easiest to stand;
  But O, my fatherland, how painful now for thee!
  There is no choice today: we suffer from all three.

ELISA

Elisa sant sijn staf den doden te doen leven,
Den staf was crachteloos, het kint is doot gebleven
  Tot dat Elisa self den doden heeft genaeckt,
  Doe heeft hem God de Heer weer levendich gemaeckt:
De wet, een harden staf aen Israël gesonden
En conde niemant doen oprysen uyt de sonden,
  God selve comen most in onse vleys en bloet
  Om ons te brengen aen soo costelijcken goet.

ELISHA

Elisha sent his staff, the dead with life to bless:
It could not raise the child: the staff was powerless.
  Elisha came himself to touch the child, and then
    The Lord sent out his power to make him live again.
The law, a rigid staff, was sent to Israel;
It could not bring new life, it could not make them well.
  But only God himself in our own flesh and blood
    Could raise us to new life and make us truly good.

NEW TESTAMENT POEMS

TWEEDE BOECK

LOF JESU CHRISTI

Ghy die Permessi vloet gaet watersuchtich lecken,
En suyselende droomt van Phoebus met sijn lier,
Cupido met zijn booch, Dione met haer vier,
Comt siet wat soeter drift tot dichten my comt wecken.
    Mijn Phoebus is de Son die t'edel hooft ging decken
Met dorenen getackt in plaets van lauwerier,
Mijn Pegasus dien Geest die met een snel geswier
Sijn vleugelen snee-wit quam over hem wtstrecken.
    Mijn Cyrrha is het bloet daer met hy ons genas,
Sijn dobbele natuyr mijn dobbele Parnas,
Sijn rietstock mijne pen, sijn adem diese drijvet.
    Sijn leven ende doot zijn t'ongemeten stof
Van mijnen soeten sanck en zijnen groten lof
Die hier begonnen wort en namaels eeuwich blijvet.

PRAISE OF JESUS CHRIST

All you who vainly seek to quench your thirst
At Hippocrene, or dream of Phoebus' lyre,
Of Cupid's bow, of Venus with her fire,
Come see what nobler muse inspires my verse.
  My Phoebus is the Sun whose head was covered
With twisted thorns and not with laurel bound,
My Pegasus that Dove whose rushing sound
Of bending, snow-white wings above him hovered.
  My Cyrrha is his blood, which makes me pure,
His double nature is my double cure,
His rod my pen, his breath my inspiration,
  His holy life and death the endless source
Of my sweet song, which here begins its course
In heaven's choir to find its consummation.

Maria

Gesegent is de maecht de croon van alle maechden,
Den tempel van Gods Soon en wesentlijcke cracht,
Den schonen dageraet waer door ons nu toe-lacht
De Sonne daer soo dick de Vaderen na vraechden.
    Geluckich, meer als die die oyt den Heer behaechden,
De suster van haer kint, de dochter van haer dracht,
De bruyt van diese self ter wereld heeft gebracht
In wiens ontfanckenis beyd' aerd' en hemel waechden.
    Wel salich sijn voorwaer haer ongeraeckte borsten
Waer na de bronne self des levens plach te dorsten:
Wel salich is den schoot daer in hy heeft gerust:
    Maer salich boven al sijn sulcke die haer leven
(Gelijck Maria dee) tot zijnen dienst begeven
En hebben in sijn woort haer hertelijcke lust.

MARY

Most blessed is this maid, all virgins' crown,
The temple of God's Son and inmost might,
The dawn through which the long-awaited light
Of heaven's rising Sun comes smiling down.
  Most blessed she, the sister of her child,
Daughter of him whom she herself gave birth,
The bride of him who from her womb came forth —
That womb where heaven and earth were reconciled.
  Most blessed are those breasts from which the spring
Of life itself lay thirsting for a drink,
Most blessed is that lap in which he lay;
  But blessed above all are those who live
(As Mary did) for him, who gladly give
Their lives to him by walking in his way.

GEBOORTE

Ick ken u wel, ô vande hel
Bestormer en verwinder,
Al legdy hier, onnosel dier
Gelijck der menschen kinder.

   Gods eeuwich Soon, wt uwen throon
Sijt ghy ons comen nader
Op dat de Heer, tot sijner eer
Mocht worden onsen Vader.

   Die noyt en paerd' u heeft gebaert,
En sonder sond' u teelde,
Op dat de vleck, en 'tvuyl gebreck
Van ons geboorte heelde.

   Ons droeven val, heeft inden stal
O Coninck u verschoven,
Dus maeckty ree, een reyne stee
Voor al die u geloven.

   Int scherpe strooy, en dempich hooy
Ligdy met cleyner lusten
Op dat een dach, mijn siele mach
Te sachtelijcker rusten.

   De winter-lucht, en 'twint-gerucht
O Jesu doet u kermen
Op dat ghy sout, mijn herte cout
In uwer liefde wermen.

NATIVITY

I know you well: you vanquished hell
As conqueror and king
Though you appear as baby here,
A poor and wormlike thing.

You left the throne, your Father's own,
To join us from above,
That God might be eternally
Our Father, through your love.

No man on earth defiled your birth,
No sin in your conception,
So that our blot by sin begot
Might turn into perfection.

Our sorry fall to dirty stall
Sent you from heaven's throne,
Thus making clean a place serene
For those who are your own.

All night you lay on pricking hay,
A crude and dusty nest,
That my soul may, one blessed day,
Find softer, sweeter rest

The air was cold, the wind was bold
O Jesu, at your birth,
That your love's art might warm my heart
And all the chilly earth.

De naare nacht, in sware clacht
Doet meerderen u pijnen
Dies mijn gesicht, het helle licht
In eeuwicheyt sal schijnen.

Het soute nat, o weerde schat
Rolt over uwe wangen
Op dat mijn ooch, van tranen drooch
Genade mocht erlangen.

U handekens, in bandekens
O heylant sijn gewonden
Op dat ick zy, verlost en vry
Van alle mijne sonden.

U lippen root, de sondaers snoot
Vertroosten also soetgens,
Der slangen cop, daer suldy op
Noch treden met u voetgens.

U oochgens reyn, al sijnse cleyn
Doorstralen alle hoecken,
Ontsienelijck, maer vriendelijck
Voor die u aenschijn soecken.

O bruydegom, weest wellecom
Ick heb u lang' gebeydet,
Oock in mijn hert, geboren werd
En nimmer van my scheydet.

The gloomy night increased your fright
And plaintive misery,
So that a bright, amazing light
Might ever shine on me.

A sweet salt tear, O Savior dear,
Makes moist your tiny face,
So that my eye, forever dry,
May sparkle with your grace.

Your little hands in little bands
Are bound as with a string,
That I may be forever free
From sin and from its sting.

Your lips of red for sinner's dread
Bring comfort sure and sweet;
The serpent's head shall be downtread
By your bedimpled feet.

Your perfect eyes, I realize,
Are small, but they can see;
For with love's grace in this dark place
They turn and look on me.

O Bridegroom small, laid in a stall,
Make glad my waiting heart;
O infant wee, be born in me
And nevermore depart.

Bondelken myrrhe

De myrrhe weert mijn Coninck wiert geschonken
Eerbiedich, doe hy inder cribben lach,
Hoewel aen hem geen luyster men en sach
Noch van gesteent' sijn clederen en bloncken.
    Den myrrhen-wijn mijn liefsten heeft gedroncken
Met bitterheyt gevoet den heelen dach
Doe hy betaeld' het droevige gelach
In diepen druck om mijnentwil gesoncken.
    In myrrhe groen mijn liefste was om-wonden
Doe in het graf, vol strepen en vol wonden,
Sijn lichaem lach bewaret voor den stanck.
    Van dese myrrh' een tuylken van dry struycken
Ick op mijn hert, ja in mijn hert wil luycken
Mijn siel tot troost, mijn lief tot eer en danck.

MYRRH-BOUQUET

A gift of myrrh was offered to my King
To honor him as in his crib he lay
Although his tiny form did not display
A royal splendor, nor his hand a ring.

Of bitter myrrh my Lover had to drink;
It was his only solace on that day
When for my load of sin he had to pay,
In deep distress for my sake had to sink.

In verdant myrrh my Lover's limbs were bound
When, full of wounds and bruises, in the ground
His body lay preserved from rank decay.

Of these three twigs a myrrh-wreath I will bind
Upon my heart, yes in my heart, and find
My comfort there, my Love his myrrh-bouquet.

KINDER-MOORT

Doe den gecroonden wolf de schaepkens nieu-geboren
Met zijnen wreeden muyl te Bethlehem verslont,
Een clagelijck geschrey steech vander aerden gront
En quam ten hemel in voor Gods gerechte oren.

Een vliegende geswerm der engelen vercoren
Omvinck den claynen hoop geplettert en doorwont,
En nam de witte siel van haren roden mont
Die stellend' onbesmet Gods aengesicht te voren.

Hoe cort was haren tijt in droevich tranen-dal!
Hoe groot is hare vreucht die eeuwich dueren sal!
Hoe loven zy den Heer haer gonstigen weldader!

Sy gingen haestelijck int leven door den doot,
Gerucket onverwacht wt hares moeders schoot,
Gedragen inden schoot van haren liefsten Vader.

MURDER OF
THE INNOCENTS

When Herod, cruel wolf in kingly guise,
Attacked the new-born lambs and murdered them,
Lamenting moans arose in Bethlehem,
Reaching God's righteous ears with their sad cries.
  A band of chosen angels, swarming down,
Embraced the heap of battered little ones,
And, taking their white souls from their red mouths,
Presented them unblemished at God's throne.
  How short the time of tears they had to bear!
How great their joy shall be forevermore!
How sweet their song to God, whom they adore!
  One hasty step through death to life and rest,
Jerking them rudely from a mother's breast,
Forever placed them in their Father's care.

Besnijdinge

Wanneer de son het vroege licht
Comt wt de blaeuwe baren
Openbaren
Indien de nevels ros en dicht
Die tsamen opwaerts varen
Hem ontclaren
So wacht u op den avont laet
Die t'seewaert of te velde gaet
Eer t'onweer comt aenswaeyen,
T'wil regenen, t'wil draeyen
Ende waeyen.

O groote Son, wt s'Vaders schoot
Die ons ter rechter tijden
Quaemt verblijden
U opganck was van bloede root
Doe ghy het swaer besnijden
Wildet lijden;
Dit was een voorboo' vande vloet
En t'storten van u dierbaer bloet
Dat ghy met suere vlagen
Opt eynde van u dagen
Soudet dragen.

CIRCUMCISION

When morning sun, its early light
Above the waves revealing,
Comes stealing
Through cloudy fogs that dim the sight,
His rosy face appealing
Concealing,
Take warning, all who hunt or sail,
This day will end in storm and gale;
The thunder will be frightening,
The rainstreaks will be brightening
Into lightning.

O holy Sun, whose dawning met
Eternity's decision
With time's precision,
Thy rising was in bloody red:
The lurid crimson vision
Of circumcision.
This was prophetic of the flood
And spilling of thy precious blood;
The God-forsaken crying,
Red sunset terrifying
Of thy dread dying.

Wanneer de Son den ronden soom
Der diep gewelfde salen
Comt te malen
Schickt hy hem inde stille stroom
Met rosen-rode stralen
Neer te dalen
Soo wacht een schonen dageraet
Die t'seewaert of te velde gaet
Waer door seer schiedelijcken
De duysterheyt moet strijcken
Ende wijcken.

Hoe root was uwen onderganck
O Jesu, als u t'leven
Wou begeven!
U open borst, u leden cranck
Men sach van bloede cleven
Ende beven.
Maer door u dodelijck geclach
Most ons den liefelijcken dach
Van Gods genade schijnen.
Ons smerten al verdwijnen
Door u pijnen.

When evening sun, the rocking rim
Of heaven's deep-arched ceiling
Revealing,
With rosy redness settles him
Into the sparkling motion
Of ocean,
Anticipate a happy dawn
On sailor's sea or hunter's lawn;
At morning's first faint sighing
The darkness will be flying
And dying.

How crimson was Thy setting sun,
O Jesu, God-forsaken,
Soul-shaken.
Thy sorry side was blood-berun,
Thy wounds with red were quivering
And shivering.
But through the crimson of thy death
For us is breathed the morning breath
Of heaven's new creation;
From thy sunset damnation
Our salvation.

SIMON PETRUS

Hoe wenschelijcken stont het in des Heeren kerck
Als Simon Petrus noch daer inne plach te leven!
   Nu isset anders niet als een verworren werck
   Want Petrus is verreyst, en Simon is gebleven.

SIMON PETER

How much improved the church would be in every way
If Simon Peter's spirit inspired it still today!
  Now nothing else is left but a confused affair,
  For Peter has departed, but Simon still is there.

JODEN

T'is wonder, Jesu (spreeckt een ongelovich Jode)
Dat ghy die sijt een mensch, u selven maeckt tot Gode:
  T'is wonder, Heere (seyt een Christ-gelovich hert)
  Dat ghy, God sijnde, mensch om mijnentwille wert.

JEWS

Amazing (says the Jew who is no child of Thine)
That you who are a man should make yourself divine;
  Amazing (says the man who gives himself to Thee)
  That you who are divine became a man for me.

Timmermans sone

Van waer comt doch de cracht aen desen wonder-dader?
En is niet (alsmen weet) een timmerman zijn vader?
  Ja, maer den Timmerman wiens Soone ghy soo laeckt
Is die het schoon gebou des hemels heeft gemaeckt.

CARPENTER'S SON

From whence proceeds the power such miracles to show?
His father was a simple carpenter, you know.
  Yes, but the Carpenter whose Son you so defy
  Is he who built the earth and the palatial sky.

SONDARESSE

O Sondaers, schouwet aen die grote sondaerinne
Die deerlijck wtgestreckt voor Christi tafel leyt;
En neemt van haer een stael der goddelijcker minne,
En siet in hem een proef van goedertierenheyt.

Haer ogen die in lust soo plegen te gaen weyen
Nu zijn geworden van sijn beenen het lampet,
Het water wt haer hooft, ô overmatich schreyen!
Heeft die gelijck een stroom wtvloeyende genett.

Dien mont waer mee sy wist de jonckheyt aen te locken
Het stof van zijne tree'n te lecken heeft gepoocht,
En met haer jeugdich haar, en met haer fiere locken
In plaetse van een dwaal zijn enckels sijn gedroocht.

Den Nardus die wel-eer haer cleederen dee ruycken
Die heeftse wtgestort op zijn gesegent vel,
Dien hals die sy soo hooch gewoon was op te luycken
Buychtse ter aerden, voor sijn voeten een schabel.

Ghy hebt, ô Herder goet dit schaepken soo elendich
In uwen trouwen schoot sachtmoedelijck ontfaen,
En watse aen u dee dat hebbet ghy inwendich
Aen haer verslagen Geest veel heerlijcker gedaen.

Sinful woman

O sinners, see this sinful woman lying
Stretched out at Jesus' feet in misery;
And see a proof of love in her sad crying,
And see in him a proof of clemency.

Her eyes, which once with sinful lust were glowing,
Have now become for him a lowly ewer;
The water from her face profusely flowing
She pours out on his limbs to make them pure.

The mouth which once enticed gay youth to pleasure
Now tries to lick the dust from off his feet;
And of her youthful hair, once her proud treasure,
She makes a towel to dry his ankles sweet.

The spices once expended on her clothing
She pours unstinted on his blessed skin:
Her neck, once her delight, becomes her loathing,
She lowers it, a footstool now for him.

Good Shepherd, you have clasped this lamb so lowly
In your kind arms and gently made her whole;
What she presented as an offering holy
You much more richly proffered to her soul.

Sy sach u, maer ghy hebt met vaderlijcke ogen
Aenschouwet haer gebreck, verlichtet haer gemoet
Sy naderde tot u, maer ghy hebtse getogen.
Sy wies u, en ghy wiescht haer siele met u bloet.

Den cus dien zy u gaf soo veel ick niet en achte
Als dien ghy haer int hert onsienlijck hebt gedruckt:
Haer balsem niet soo weert als daer ghy mee versachte
Haer wonden, wt den doot haer hebbende geruckt.

Sy droochde neerstelijck u onbevleckte leden,
En ghy hebt afgedroocht van tranen haer aenschijn
Haer gevend' uwen troost: en lietse gaen in vreden
Versekert datse sou een kint des hemels sijn.

O vrouwe, ghy hebt sterck en vierichlijck beminnet,
Veel sonden u de Heer op eenmael oock vergaf
Wiens onverdiende liefd' ons feylen overwinnet
Op dat van zijnen dienst wy nimmer laten af.

She looked at you, but with your eyesight pure
You saw her weaknesses and made her good.
She came to you, but you it was who drew her;
She washed you, but you washed her with your blood.

The kiss she gave to you is not a treasure
Like that with which you kissed her heart unseen;
The balsam which she poured knows not the measure
Of that which cured her wounds and made her clean.

She wiped your perfect limbs with her long tresses,
But you have wiped the tears from off her face;
She went her way in peace, freed from distresses,
Forevermore a child of heaven's grace.

O woman, you have loved with fiery spirit;
Many the sins the Lord forgave for you!
Our failures are all covered by his merit
That we may never cease his will to do.

Lijden christi

Des werelts rond' te gronden op een Niet,
Het woeste meyr te dwingen in sijn palen,
Der sonnen rat doen rijsen en doen dalen
Sijn teyckens van een eyndeloos gebiet.

Noch meer is dit, ô Jesu, dat ghy liet
Om sondaers vuyl des hemels reyne salen,
En hare schult onschuldich quaemt betalen
In helsche quael en dodelijck verdriet.

Och! costen wy te recht dit wonder smaken!
Wat steen-rots sou niet als een oven blaken!
Wat hert sou niet met liefde sijn doorwont!

Maer neen, geen mensch, geen engel can het vaten;
Ghy Heer alleen cont het ons weten laten,
Want ghy alleen sijt die het ondervondt.

Suffering of christ

From nothing to bring forth the round creation,
To force the raging sea to keep his bounds,
The rising and the setting sun his rounds —
These are the signs of endless domination.
    But greater still, O Christ, that you should leave
The spotless halls of heaven for sinners' filth,
Debtless to pay their debts from your great wealth
In hellish agony and deadly grief.
    O, could we rightly fathom this great feat!
What stony rock would then not melt with heat!
What heart would not with love be wounded through!
    But no; no man nor angel, Lord, can know it;
You, Lord, alone to us can ever show it,
For none has ever known this pain but you.

Avond-mael

O spijse die ons uyt den hemel is gegeven!
O dranck die eens gesmaeckt den smaeck vermeeren doet!
O spijse die ons tot int ander leven voedt!
O dranck die crachtelijck de doden geeft het leven!
O spijse die ons niet laet aende aerde cleven
Maer proeven dat de Heer is liefelijck en soet!
O milden hemels-dou, veel beter als de vloet
Die wt den harden steen was eenmael opgedreven!
O Manna, af gedaelt van Godes hoge hant!
O soeten druyven-tros wt het beloofde lant
Vervult mijn hert en mont met uwen lof en prijse.
Climt opwaerts, ô mijn siel, dit sichtbare verlaet,
T'is uwen bruydegom die u alleen versaet
Wiens bloet is waerlijck dranck, wiens vleys is waerlijck
spijse.

THE LORD'S SUPPER

O holy food sent down to us from heaven!
O drink which, tasted, makes us long for more!
O food by which we grow to heaven's door!
O drink that to the dead new life has given!
  O food that clings not to the lowly earth
But makes us taste that Christ is sweet and good!
Mild heaven-dew, far better than the flood
That out of the hard rock was once brought forth!
  O Manna, dropping down from God's high **hand!**
Cluster of grapes from out the promised land,
Fill both my heart and mouth with praises sweet.
  Climb up, my soul, forsake that which you see,
Thy bridegroom is the only food for thee:
His blood is truly wine, his flesh is truly meat.

Voet-wasschinge

Ist wonder dat de Heer sijn clederen afleyt
Die hem ontcledet self van zijne heerlijcheyt?
Ist wonder dat hy neemt een lijwaet hem te gorden,
Die knecht, om onsentwil, van meester is geworden?
Ist wonder dat hy wascht zijn iongeren den voet,
Die noch sou reynigen haer siele met zijn bloet?

Foot-washing

Why wonder that he doffed his garments willingly,
Who had unclothed himself of heavenly majesty?
Why wonder that he tied a towel round his waist,
Who, for our sakes, as Master, assumed a servant's place?
Why wonder that he washed the feet of humble men,
Who later with his blood would wash away their sin?

Bloedige sweet

Trage siel, die in my slaept
Geeut en gaept,
Wilt u bruygom niet vergeten.
Waket op, en comt hem dra
Volgen na
Inden hof van Oliveten.

Siet hoe hem u Schepper buckt,
Onderdruckt
Door u eysselijcke sonden.
Siet hoe hem sijn teere huyt
Berstet wt
In wel duysent-duysent wonden.

Ah! sijn sweet is enckel bloet,
Met een vloet
Stralende van sijne leden
Ah! de aerde drinckt haer sat
In het nat
Sijpende van zijne treden.

En my dunckt dat ick aenschou
Desen dou
Opwaerts inde bladen trecken;
Was t'angierken niet snee-wit,
Dat nu sit
Oversaeyt met bonte plecken?

Bloody Sweat

Lazy soul, why yawn so deep,
Gape and sleep?
Waken now and follow me.
See, your Bridegroom now has gone
To the lone
Garden of Gethsemane.

See how your Creator weeps,
Bends, and creeps
Underneath your load of sin.
A thousand-thousand crimson tears
Trickle here
From his tearing, bursting skin.

Ah, his sweat is really blood,
Like a flood,
Streaming forth from every limb.
All the earth can drink her fill,
If she will,
Of those drops that fall from him.

When I look, I notice, too,
That this dew
Colors stem and leaf and bud.
That carnation once snow-white
Now is bright
With dark spots of crimson blood.

T'blonde roosken gloeyt sijn schoot
Sangels-root;
En de bleecke Tulibanten
Sijn verkeert (of droomtet my?)
Op de ry
In gemengde flamboyanten.

Maer een bloem int duyre bloet
Opgevoet
Sie ick wter aerden comen;
O hoe liefelijcken bloem!
Die den roem
Allen cruyden heeft benomen.

Godes milde goedicheyt
Wtgebreyt
Over die de sonden rouwen
Is haer alder-soetste naem,
Hullepsaem
Diese met geloof aenschouwen.

Droeve siel, die in my weent,
Sucht en steent
Wilt dees bloeme niet vergeten;
Ider hofken dat ghy siet
Draechtse niet
Maer den hof van Oliveten.

That white rose now shoots a bud
Red as blood,
Those pale tulips, in their turn,
Are transformed (Is it not so?)
Row by row,
And like bright flamboyants burn.

But what is that flower fair
Springing there
From this holy, bloody ground?
Lovely flower that will replace
By its grace
All the flowers that can be found?

"Jesus' goodness and his love,
Spread above
All who sorrow for their sin"
Is its name, surpassing sweet,
Rich, replete,
Healing balm for helpless men.

Sorry soul, which in me moans,
Grieves, and groans,
Keep this flower in memory.
Do not seek it everywhere,
Only there:
Garden of Gethsemane.

Petri tranen

O ganck vermengt met swerven ende swieren!
O vrees' en hoop die quellet mijn gemoet!
O vier dat my die siele branden doet!
O ogen, niet meer ogen maer rivieren!
　　O yver blint die u niet liet bestieren,
Maer roekeloos deedt treden mijnen voet
In dit gewest, daer mijnes Heeren bloet
Wort na getracht van dees verwoede dieren!
　　O tonge die mijn tong' tot leugen dreeft!
O hanen-craey waer door my t'herte beeft!
Wat troost cont ghy my troosteloos verlenen?
　　O Jesu, die voor my dit lijden smaeckt,
Wiens weerden naem ick drymael heb versaeckt
Staet eenmael stil, en siet mijn bitter wenen.

PETER'S TEARS

O swaying steps, uncertain of your going!
O fear and hope that melt my heart with shame!
O fire that makes my soul a burning flame!
O eyes, no longer eyes but rivers flowing!
　O blind bravado, lacking all direction,
Leading my reckless feet into this room
Where these wild beasts prepare my Master's doom,
Thirsting to lick the blood of his perfection!
　O girlish tongue that drove my tongue to lying!
O rooster-crow that tears my soul apart!
What cheer have you to give my cheerless heart?
　O Jesu, tasting anguish for my crimes,
Whose worthy name I have denied three times,
Stand still just once and see my bitter crying.

SIJN BLOET SY OVER ONS ENDE ONSE KINDEREN

Het geen u vyant riep tot zijn verderf en schade
Dat roep ick tot u oock, ô heylant vol genade,
   Maer tot mijn salicheyt, in vieriger aendacht;
    U bloet zy over my en over mijn geslacht.
U bloet sy over my, mijn sonden te versmoren,
En op mijn kinderen, om t'quaet haer aengeboren
   Te wasschen, en haer siel te redden van gepijn.
    Soo sal der Joden vloeck voor ons een segen zijn.

His blood be on us and our children

That which thy foes called down as curse upon their race,
That also I call down, O Savior full of grace,
  As blessing, not as curse, I beg this now anew:
  May thy blood be on me and on my children, too.
Thy blood be over me to smother all my sin
And over all my own their righteousness to win;
  To wash away their guilt, to set their spirits free —
  The Jewish curse will be a blessing then for me.

HY DROECH
ONSE SMERTEN

T'en zijn de Joden niet, Heer Jesu, die u cruysten,
Noch die verradelijck u togen voort gericht,
Noch die versmadelijck u spogen int gesicht,
Noch die u knevelden, en stieten u vol puysten,
    T'en sijn de crijchs-luy niet die met haer felle vuysten
Den rietstock hebben of den hamer opgelicht,
Of het vervloecte hout op Golgotha gesticht,
Of over uwen rock tsaem dubbelden en tuyschten:
    Ick bent, ô Heer, ick bent die u dit heb gedaen,
Ick ben den swaren boom die u had overlaen,
Ick ben de taeye streng daermee ghy ginct gebonden,
    De nagel, en de speer, de geessel die u sloech,
De bloet-bedropen croon die uwen schedel droech:
Want dit is al geschiet, eylaes! om mijne sonden.

HE BORE OUR GRIEFS

No, it was not the Jews who crucified,
Nor who betrayed you in the judgment place,
Nor who, Lord Jesus, spat into your face,
Nor who with buffets struck you as you died.
No, it was not the soldiers fisted bold
Who lifted up the hammer and the nail,
Or raised the cursèd cross on Calvary's hill,
Or, gambling, tossed the dice to win your robe.
I am the one, O Lord, who brought you there,
I am the heavy cross you had to bear,
I am the rope that bound you to the tree,
The whip, the nail, the hammer, and the spear,
The blood-stained crown of thorns you had to wear:
It was my sin, alas, it was for me.

Coperen slange

Geswollen vant fenijn der dodelijcker slangen,
Voorsmakende het vier dat nimmermeer en blust
Wy sleepten langs de gront, en hadden geene rust
Ter tijt toe dat tot u wy keerden onse gangen.

O slange sonder gift, die voor ons opgehangen
De welverdiende grim ws Vaders hebt gesust:
Ghy geeft ons het geloof, waer door wy met een lust
Omvingen uwen troost en sijn van u omvangen.

Ghy quamet onse sond' ontsonden en bedelven,
Ghy namet onse quael en loedtse op u selven,
Ghy wiert voor ons een worm getreden met den voet.

Treckt ons tot u om hooch, en leert ons recht bedencken
Hoe ghy der slangen hooft cost morselen en crencken
Doort breken van u lijf, doort storten van u bloet.

Brazen serpent

Swollen with venom of the deadly snake,
Hot as the hellish flames that never cease,
We dragged along the ground and found no peace
Until we saw thee dying for our sake.
  O fangless serpent, hanging on the tree,
Soft'ning for us the grimness of God's face,
Thou giv'st the faith by which we dare embrace
Thy holy cure, and be embraced by thee.
  Our sin, now sinless, thou hast come to bury,
Our sickness loaded on thyself to carry,
Become a worm down-trodden with the foot.
  O draw us up to thee, teach us to feel
How thou hast crushed the serpent with thy heel
By offering for us thy flesh and blood.

Doot christi

O leven onser siel, ô Vorst vant eeuwich leven,
O die het leven self den doden hebt gegeven,
  Hoe hebdy vande doot u leven niet verlost!
  Wie hadde oyt gemeynt dat God oock sterven cost?

T'selve

Plichtancker onser hoop, steenrotse vant betrouwen,
Afgrond' van onse liefd' in wien wy sijn behouwen,
  Ghy sijtet die de doot al stervende verwon.
  Hoe! wie vermoede dat de doot oock sterven con?

DEATH OF CHRIST

O life of every soul, O life's eternal Head,
O you who life itself have given to the dead,
  How is it that the depths of death you wished to try?
  Who would have ever thought that even God could die?

THE SAME

True anchor of our hope, firm pillar of our trust,
Abyss of all our love, in whom we are made just,
  By dying once for all, death's power you defy.
  Who would have ever thought that even death could die?

VEGE-VIER

O ongeluckich mensch, die na u droeve jaren
U rekeninge maeckt noch in een vier te varen,
   En troost u, dat ghy na voldoening' van u schult
   Ten langen lesten eens daer wt geraken sult.
Ghy sijt, ghy sijt te verr' verbijstert wten wege.
Ah! stiert u siel om hoog', en waechtse niet om lege.
   Want ick veel stappen sie die na beneden staen,
   Maer geene die van daer weerom na boven gaen.

PURGATORY

Unlucky men you are, who after life's sad story
Still must anticipate the fires of purgatory.
  You hope that when your share of punishment has passed,
  At last you will escape from there — at longest last.
You walk, you walk too far along this way of woe;
Direct your soul on high, instead of down below.
  For I see many steps descend into the pit,
  But none, that I can see, ascending out of it.

CORT GEBET

Het goede wilt ons, Heer, toemeten,
T'sy dat wij 't bidden, of vergeten.
  Het quade geeft ons nimmermeer
  Al baden wy het noch soo seer.

SHORT PRAYER

Give us the good, O Lord, we pray,
Whether we ask it or forget.
  And keep the evil far away
  No matter how we ask for it.

GEBET DES MIDDAECHS

Het vierich stralen vande son
Opt hoochste sien wy rijsen
O dat de sonne spreken con!
Sijn schepper sou hy prijsen.

Ghy sonne der gerechticheyt
Comt onse siele vanden
Die in een coude flaeute leyt,
En doetse vierich branden.

Geeft datse gans versmelten mach
In Goddelijcker minnen
En diese eer te haten plach
Mach jonstelijck besinnen.

Den acker vant vervrosen hert
Wilt coesteren en stercken
Op dattet weerom vruchtbaer werd'
In deuchdelijcke wercken.

Tot dat wy werden ingeleyt
Wt duysternis en pijnen
Daer ghy en wy in eeuwicheyt
Als sonnen sullen schijnen.

Prayer at Noonday

The fiery sun has reached his peak —
We see his flashes blazing.
O if the sun could only speak!
His God he would be praising.

O holy sun of righteousness,
See how our souls are yearning!
Light up their chilly dreariness
And start the fires burning.

Grant that our souls may melt away
In godly consecration;
Instead of hating, that they may
Show love and dedication.

The acre of the frozen heart
Needs nurturing and tending;
O make the fruitful branches start
With virtues never-ending.

Till we shall all be led away
From darkness and repining,
With thee in that eternal day
As suns forever shining.

VIER PAUSEN

Leo, Clement, Urbaen, en Pouwel
T'saem rechten op den woesten grouwel.
Pouwel, Clement, Leo, Urbaen
Hebben Gods kerck veel leets gedaen.
Leo, Urbaen, Pouwel, Clement
Sijn vande waerheyt afgewent.
Urbaen, Clement, Pouwel, en Leeu
Waren vier plagen van haer eeu.

FOUR POPES

Leo, Clement, Urban, Paul —
Wicked persecutors all.
Paul and Clement, Leo, Urban
To God's church were all disturbin'.
Leo, Urban, Paul, Clement
Took the way that error went.
Urban, Clement, Paul, and Leo
Brought their age to misereo.

Vier leeraers

Luther, Philips, Calvijn, en Beze
Leerden de waerheyt en Gods vrese.
Beze, Philips, Calvijn, en Luther
Maeckten den Paus tot een sant-ruyter.
Beze, Calvijn, Luther, Philipp'
Staen onbeweget als een clipp'.
Luther, Philips, Beze, Calvijn
Gods hooch-verlichte dienaers zijn.

FOUR PREACHERS

Luther, Calvin, Beza, Knox
Made their churches orthodox.
Knox and Beza, Calvin, Luth'
Left the pope to tell the truth.
Calvin, Luther, Knox, and Bez'
Stand secure from error's ways.
Beza, Luther, Knox, and Calvin
In God's truth are always delvin'.

OTHER POEMS

OVERIGE GEDICHTEN

Secten

Twee geesten onder ons den Salichmaker quellen,
De eene soude gaern in twijfel willen stellen
   Dat hy is ware mensch: de ander drijft den spot
   Daermede datmen seyt dat hy is eeuwich Godt.
Eylaes! hoe soude doch het lant niet qualijck varen
Daer Christus wort gecruyst tusschen twee moordenaren?

SECTS

Two spirits in our day attack the Christ anew:
The one is trying to invalidate the view
  That he is truly man; the other thinks it odd
  That anyone could say he is eternal God.
Alas! how can a land expect to prosper when
It crucifies the Christ between two thieves again?

Van een medecijn

De crancke waren bly als sy u comen sagen
O Doctor, die haer trockt wt dodelijcke vlagen.
  Noch blijder was de doot als sy u had gevelt
  Wiens const soo dickmael had gebroken haer gewelt.
Maer ghy waert alderblijdst, als ghy den doot bedrogen
En wt haer clauwen waert ten hemel opgevlogen,
  Alwaer ghy rustelijck en sonder moeyte leeft
  Een leven daer die doot geen vatten aen en heeft.

EPITAPH
OF A DOCTOR

The sick were filled with joy when you came to their bed,
For often you could cure when they were almost dead.
  More joyful still was death when she had laid you low,
  Whose skill so often broke the power of her blow.
But yours the greatest joy: outwitting death's demand
And slipping from her claws, you flew to God's right hand,
  Where carefree you enjoy the rest that is your due
  And live where death no more can get a grip on you.

Van een degelijcke vrouwe

Hier rust ick soetjens inden Heer
Een vrou begaeft met deucht en eer.
Wie dat ick ben, of hoe ick hiet
(Ist mogelijck) en vraecht my niet.
Nooyt maeckt' ick garen lang' gerel.
Het swijgen past de vrouwen wel.

OF A VIRTUOUS WOMAN

Here in the Lord I sweetly rest
With meekness, grace, and honor blest.
My name or my identity
(If possible) don't ask of me.
In talk I never did excel:
Silence suits a woman well.

Van een deuchtsaem man

Hier legg' ick in mijn moeders schoot
Een vrient der vromen totten doot.
Mijn naem, mijn stam, mijn ouderdom,
Ick bidde (op soo goet weerom)
Datmen my daer mee niet en quel.
Het swijgen past de doden wel.

OF A VIRTUOUS MAN

Here in my mother's lap I rest,
A friend to all who were oppressed.
My age, my family tree, my name,
I beg (and promise you the same)
That you won't bother me to tell:
Silence suits a dead man well.

Van een droncken wijf

Hier onder slaept de droncken Beel
Diet alles iagde door de keel.
Het vaetjen dat haer vreugde gaf
Staet wtgehouwen op haer graf.
Dat sy haer man en haer geslacht
Heeft totten bedelsack gebracht
En geeft haer geen becommernis,
Maer, dat het vaetjen ledich is.

OF A DRUNKEN WIFE

Beneath this stone lies Gertie Vleer,
Who spent her life in drinking beer.
The earthen mug that made her gay
Stands graven on her tomb today.
Her husband, begging on the street,
Her children with no food to eat
Cause no grief to Gertie Vleer —
But that the mug contains no beer.

VAN EEN LUYAERT

Hier rust de luye Melis Brant.
Wat seg' ick? 'tis een misverstant:
Hoe can te rusten sijn geseyt
Die nooyt en heeft gearrebeyt?

OF A LAZYBONES

Here rests the lazy Melis Brand.
Here rests? That's hard to understand:
Here rests, is not the thing to say
Of one who never worked a day.

SPREUKEN DER SEVEN WIJSE

Was al de werelt dwaes behalven seven wijsen,
Waer mede conden sy haer wijsheyt dan bewijsen?
  Want, of haer eygen mont toeschreef haer desen prijs,
  (En die zich selven roemt en is voorwaer niet wijs)
Of t'volgt dat zy (het welck een saeck is om te spotten)
Wijs zijn geweest alleen na t'oordeel vande sotten.

Proverbs of the Seven Sages

If all the world were fools except for seven sages,
How could they ever prove their wisdom to the ages?
   For either their own mouths assigned themselves the prize
   (And they who praise themselves are never really wise),
Or else the case must be (and that would break all rules)
That they were only wise according to the fools.

Antwoort

De wijsen hebben daer haer wijsheyt mee bewesen
Dat niemant van haer al voor wijs wou sijn gepresen.
  De sotten hebben daer haer sotheyt mee verraen
  Dat niemant van haer al voor sot en wilde gaen.

Answer

How do wise men reveal their wisdom to men's eyes?
By having no desire to be considered wise.
  But foolish men betray their folly by this rule:
  Not one of them admits that he might be a fool.

OP DE CANONIZATIE
VAN IGNATIUS LOYOLA

Wie heeft Ignatium doch gecanonizeret?
De Paus en isset niet die hem soo heeft ge-eret
 (Hoewel het menich meynt) noch die sijn beeltenis
 Verhieven in de kerck, noch die de eerste mis
In zijn capelle dee'n: maer t'waren de soldaten,
Die, als sijn cameraets, haer hebben horen laten,
 En hebben hem gestelt in desen hogen stant.
 Want als sy over al dees nieu-gebacken Sant
Met schieten van c a n o n op haer manier vereerden
Doe docht haer dat sy hem eerst recht c a n o n i z e e r d e n.

ON THE CANONIZATION
OF IGNATIUS OF LOYOLA

Who was it canonized the saint Ignatius?
Some think it was the Pope who was so gracious!
  But no! Nor those who raised his statue overhead,
  Nor those who in his chapel first served the holy bread.
  It was the soldiers who decided it was time
  Their comrade should ascend into the saintly line.
And when their *cannons* roared with mighty intonation,
That really was the day of his *canonization*.

Voor...
MARIA SCHUYRMANS

Doe Schuyrmans kint ontfangen had het leven
De eer, de const, de schoonheyt, en de deucht
Poogden om strijt wie hare groene jeucht
Tot gesellin van God sou zijn gegeven.

De een' haer wou tot inden doot aencleven,
De ander haer beloofde gonst en vreucht,
Des eens geluck scheen d'anders ongeneucht,
T'en waer dat God t' verschil had opgeheven.

Dochters, sprack hy, t'en is voorwaer geen ree'n
Dat elck van u bewoon een huys alleen:
Dies last ick u dat ghy tesaam verdraget.

Dit wierd' gedaen, en sonder veel beraets
Sy hebben altegaer genomen plaets
(Gelijck wy sien) in dese soete maget.

For...
MARIA SCHUYRMANS

When Anne Marie, Van Schuyrman's child, was born,
Honor and wisdom, beauty, grace, and truth
Struggled to gain from God, in her green youth,
The right to be companion to her form.

One promised she would cling to her till death,
Another offered favor, peace, and joy;
But what would make one happy would annoy
The others all, till God devised this plan:

Daughters, there is no need, he wisely said,
That each of you should have a house apart;
So live in peace, as I command you to.

And this was done; with little more ado
They moved together into her young heart,
To dwell (as we can see) in this sweet maid.

TREUR-DICHT

O Charon, die bevaert alleen de stille veeren,
En legdy nimmermeer aen ancker uwe schuyt?
Ist altijt af en aen? ist altijt in en wt?
En sleypty altijt mee diemen niet can ontbeeren?
   Sochty gemeyne vracht, wat conde het ons deren?
Daer leeft soo menich eer-en-redeloos schavuyt,
Haelt die in uwen boot, set die in u cajuyt,
Maer en ontvoert ons niet de goe Nassousche Heeren.
   Ghy hebt t'onrechter tijt Ernst Casimir gelae'n.
Wy kennent niet voor goet, wy connent niet verstaen.
Wat seg' ick? ben ick in mijn hersenen geslagen?
   'tIs Charon noch sijn schip dat met hem hene-vaert,
Ten hemel geldt de reys, hy climt te Gode-waert,
En daer ick hem op sie het is Elias wagen.

ELEGY

O Charon, as alone you sail the silent Styx,
O, will you never drop your anchor down below?
Forever in and out? Forever to and fro?
Forever dragging off the men we cannot miss?
If you sought common freight, we would not care at all:
There are so many rogues, so many worthless louts;
Fetch them in your grim boat, force them to ferry out,
But do not take away the Princes of Nassau.
It is an evil time to rob us of our Prince;
We will not stand for it, we cannot see the sense.
What are these words I speak? Have I gone raving mad?
That is not Charon's boat that sweeps him from my sight.
This journey leads to heaven, this chariot of light
Is like Elijah's coach: it leads him home to God.

Treur-dicht

Het vier dat door u hooft den cogel heeft gedreven
O groote Casimir, doet met een coude gloet
Bevriesen, en met een versmelten onse bloet,
En in een ogenblick ons sweeten ende beven.
    De tongen tot u lof soo yverich begeven
Die uwen eelen naam voor desen was soo soet
Sijn of geheel verstomt, of bitterder als roet
Betreurende 'tverlies van u grootdadich leven.
    De aerde, die het gout draecht in haer ingewant,
Ontsluytet haeren schoot voort afgelechte pant.
Den hemel (u bereyt soo lange wijl te voren)
    Bidt dat u siele coom vermeeren haeren schijn:
Belovende dat het al helden sullen sijn
Die onder dees Planeet oyt sullen zijn geboren.

ELEGY

The fire that drove the bullet through your head
Brings a cold flame, beloved Casimir;
It melts our blood, yet freezes us with fear;
It makes us shiver while it makes us sweat.
The tongues which were so busy with your praise
And found the taste of your great name so sweet
Are either dumb or bitter with defeat,
Mourning the loss of your praiseworthy ways.
The earth, whose bowels bear a wealth of gold,
Unlocks her lap for your discarded mold.
The heavens, long preparing for this morn,
Beg for your soul to grace their panoply
And promise none but heroes it shall be
Who under this new Planet shall be born.

TREUR-DICHT

Als Casimir, u lijck gestreckt lach op de bare,
Veel dagen achter een beschreyde u de lucht
Met menich groven traen, en met soo naar gesucht
Dat het geberchte stont en daverde van vare.

Het bondich Nederlant, bestolpt met dese mare
Int midden vande seeg' verkeerde het gerucht
Van haren vreugden-rey in enckel ongenucht,
En tooch den lauwer-hoet van haren blonden hare.

Maer Vrieslant in geween wtputte al haer breyn.
Soo menich oog' daer was soo menigen fonteyn.
Die vloten onder een, en, hebbende gesworen

De doot van Casimir te wreken, spanden aen
Met al de baren van den woesten Oceaen
Om, waer het mogelijk, heel Spanjen te versmoren.

ELEGY

Your corpse, stretched out in death, O Casimir,
Caused many days of mourning in the skies,
Whose doleful weeping and whose bitter sighs
Made the high hills reverberate with fear.
United Netherlands, struck with despair,
Turned suddenly from songs of victory
Into the midst of deepest agony
And tore the laurel-hat from her blond hair.
But Friesland's people poured out all their brine.
Their weeping eyes became so many springs,
Which ran together. Swearing in their pain
Their Prince's death to avenge, they joined their motion
With all the waves of the tumultuous ocean,
If possible, to drown out all of Spain.

Princen-lof

Verenicht Nederlant, indien ghy wilt doen maken
Een wtgelesen beelt ter eeren vanden Prins,
Ghy hoeft (gelooft my) niet te lopen hier en gins
Om aen een constenaar na uwen sin te raken.
Praxiteles mach hier sijn wetenschap wel staken,
Geen Myron can voldoen ten vollen uwen wins,
Ia Daedalus is daer te slecht toe eenichsins
Al goot hy aensichten die schenen datse spraken.
Die meesters, met haer werck, hoe wonderlijck gedaen,
Sijn alle door den tijt gesleten en vergaen.
Wilt dan voor onsen Vorst tot danckbaerheyt verheffen
Het beeltenis het welck hij selve met de snee
Sijns degens heeft gewracht int jaer van dertich-twee.
Geen beytel noch pinceel soo wel hem connen treffen.

PRINCE'S PRAISE

O Netherlands, in hoping to acquire   .
A perfect statue honoring your Prince,
You need not search to find a sculptor, since
No art nor skill can do what you desire.
    Praxiteles would find his art too weak,
No Myron could fulfill your order well,
And even Daedalus were sure to fail
Although his statues seemed to live and speak.
    Those masters with their work, although sublime,
Have all been worn away by passing time.
If of our Prince you want an image true,
    No sculptor's knife or chisel could afford
Such grandeur as he cut with his own sword
In the great victory of 'thirty-two.

Oorloch

Wie is hy die het schip van Nederlant can stieren
Als onsen Admirael? hy kent de Noorder as,
Hy weet de diepten, en de streken vant compas,
Hy siet de haven al eer hy den schoot gaet vieren.

Derf Brabant tegen hem noch spartelen en tieren,
Comt haer sijn vriendelijck aenbieden niet te pas,
Hy sal, en twyfelt niet, de bootschap haer wel ras
Aenseggen met den mont van vlammende mortieren.

Vaer voort, Prins Frederick, den wieroock vant canon
Laet tot des vyants schrick benevelen de son
Terwijle wy tot God opclimmen in gebede;

Versekert, dat, gelijck een fellen donderslach
Het onweer stilt, wanneer 't niet anders wesen mach,
Alsoo den oorloch ons aenbrengen moet den vrede.

War

Who else can steer the ship of Netherlands
Besides our Admiral? He knows the North,
He knows the deeps and guides the ship to port
With compass steady, rudder in his hands.
    If Brabant dares to murmur or complain,
Not well contented with his friendly offer,
He will not hesitate his terms to proffer
By way of cannon's mouth and mortar's flame.
    Move on, Prince Fred'rick, let your cannons flash;
Let smoke like incense cloud the sunny air,
While we are climbing up to God in prayer,
    Assured that as a fearful thunder crash
Can still the storm when nought else brings surcease,
Just so the stroke of war must bring us peace.

Beelt des princen

Het gout, wiens mogentheyt soo hoge is gevlogen
Dat yder het byna aenbiddet als zijn Heer
Is merckelijck aen dien verbonden, die wel-eer
Het wt den swarten gront der aerden heeft getogen:
   Maer watten danckbaerheyt ist schuldich u te toogen
O Prins, door wien het rijst tot dese nieuwe eer
Dat het u wapenen mach voeren, en, noch meer,
U voorhooft, uwen mont, u minnelijcke oogen!
   Ick achte dat den arm die wracht dit costel werck
Wiert vlugger als een veer, en als een yser sterck
Al was hy van te voor met moedicheyt bevangen.
   En dat het edel gout wiert sacht gelijck een was,
Ja daer in wenschte te veranderen, om ras
En op het suyverste dien stempel te ontfangen.

Image of the Prince

How strange that gold, which has so great a worth
That people pray to it as to a god,
Should really owe a debt of gratitude
To those who dug it up from the black earth.
  But how its gratitude should then arise
To you, O Prince, who lift it to new fame:
That it may bear your arms, your noble name,
And even more, your forehead, mouth, and eyes!
  The hand that shaped this plaque must have become
Swift as a feather, stronger than a stone,
Although fatigued before it took this task.
  The noble gold became as soft as wax,
Yes, changed to wax, to take with instant grace
A perfect, pure impression of your face.

TRANEN-VLOET

Een wolcxken, seer gering' int aensien, onverwachtet
Geresen wttet Noort na onsen hemel clom,
Den troostelosen hoop der vromen wellecom
Maer by Gods vyanden gesmadet en verachtet.

Het spreyde sich, en smeet (wie meynde het? wie dachtet?)
Haer scharen met gewelt van blixem om end' om,
Dat Duytschlant als een see aen alle boorden swom,
En laefde menich hert in droefenis versmachtet.

Van donder het rumoer, van hagel het gecraeck
Dee trillen in haer nest den Arent en den Draeck.
Maer, o onwissen troost van dit ellendich leven!

Dien strael die allen schroom wt onse herten nam
Is wederom gekeert van daer hy henen quam.
Het licht is wechgegaan, en 'tonweer is gebleven.

Flood of tears

We saw a cloud, quite small, appearing unexpected,
Arising from the North, ascending in our sky,
Most welcome to the dying hopes of piety,
But by God's enemies derided and rejected.
   It spread itself and struck (who ever would have said?)
The enemy with strokes like lightning to the ground,
The Germans saw a sea arising all around,
Refreshing many hearts which yearned in woeful dread.
   The clamor of the thunder, spatter of the hail
Stirred up the Eagle's nest and shook the Dragon's tail.
But, O, deceitful life that turns our hopes to pains!
   That beam, which freed our hearts from all their grievous
                                 fear,
Has only risen once, again to disappear:
The light has gone away, the thunder still remains.

TRANEN-VLOET

Sal ick met mijne stem, o hogen roem der Sweden,
Wtmeten na waardy u sinne-rijck beleyt,
U ongecroockte trou, u Godesdiensticheyt,
De macht van uwen arm, 'tgewicht van uwe reden?
    De glants van u gesicht, de schoonheyt uwer leden,
U vaderlijcke gonst den goeden nooyt ontseyt,
U herte dat nooyt Prins of crijger heeft gevleyt,
U dweegen ommeganck, u minnelijcke seden?
    Hoe ghy den roden Draeck gevat hebt by den neck,
Hoe ghy den Arent wreet gekneuset hebt den beck,
Hoe u noch noot noch doot heeft connen overwinnen;
    O watten wyden meyr toont hem voor mijn gesicht!
Legt om het roer, en kiest de haven, o mijn dicht,
Datmen niet eynden can is dwaesheyt te beginnen.

FLOOD OF TEARS

Should my weak voice, O honored Swedish king,
Attempt your wealth of wisdom to assess,
Your undisputed trust, your godliness,
Your mighty arm, your weighty reasoning;
    Your noble limbs, the luster of your face,
Your kindly father-love for all the good,
Your heart, which princes' flattery withstood,
Your sweet companionship, your charm and grace;
    How you have caught the Dragon by the neck,
Have bruised and crushed the angry Eagle's beak,
How over you, nor need nor death could win:
    What mighty seas I then would have to roam!
Turn round and choose the harbor, O my poem!
What you can never end is foolish to begin.

DANCKBAERHEYT

Aenschout, genadich Vorst, hoe, om te laten blijcken
De liefde uwes naems, het danckbaer Vaderlant
Soo menich huys bynae soo menich baken brant,
En niemant zijn gebuyr in vreugde denckt te wijcken.
  De aerd' in desen nacht den hemel schijnt te lijcken
Die cierlijck boven ons sijn blaeuwe tente spant
Opt schoonste oversaeyt met menich diamant,
En heerlijcker als oyt sijn rijckdommen laet kijcken.
  Maer wilt, als ghy dit siet, o Prins van hogen moet,
Ten hemel alte-haest niet keren uwen voet,
Maeckt rekening' by ons noch lange te verbeyden:
  Dewijl de borgers van soo veel vermaerde stee'n
Met sulcken menichte van lichten, hier benee'n
Als een cleyn Hemelrijck u soecken te bereyden.

THANKFULNESS

See how, O gracious Prince, to spread the favor
Of your loved name, in grateful Netherlands
In every house a burning candle stands,
Each trying to outshine his joyful neighbor.
  The earth tonight looks like the very heaven,
Who regally above us spreads his tents,
Most graciously bedecked with diamonds:
Greatest display his wealth has ever given.
  But when you see this sight, please do not set
Your hasty steps, O Prince, toward heaven yet,
But stay with us for years before you go:
  Since burghers of the towns throughout the land
With such a multitude of lights have planned
A tiny heaven here for you below.

Het nodichst eerst

Jan Melis trout een ionge meyt,
Maer hy en heeft niet overleyt
Wat hy voor haer en hem van noot heeft.
Want hy en heeft noch cous noch schoen,
Noch cost, noch const om haer te voen.
Hy coopt het vleys al-eer hy broot heeft.

FIRST THINGS FIRST

Melis married a young girl
But forgot to plan ahead:
Not a job that he could do,
Not a stocking, not a shoe,
Not a table nor a bed —
He bought the flesh before the bread.

Aenden berisper

Berisper van mijn dicht, dit woort laet ick u weten:
Schaft beter spijs' als ick en nodicht mij ten eten,
   Of nemet mijn onthael, sulck als het is, int goe,
   Of laet mij ongemoeyt, en hout u snater toe.

TO MY BELITTLER

Belittler of my verse, this word I leave for you:
Serve better food than mine, and let me taste it, too,
  Or call my offering, such as it is, well done,
  Or leave me undisturbed, and hold your snippy tongue.

NOTES *to the Poems*

Page 39

L. 4. Music-hole: the sound-hole, for which Revius uses the word *roosken*. The single sound-hole can represent both sun and moon since they do not appear in the sky simultaneously.

Page 45

Revius entitles this poem "The Same," referring to the preceding poem, "Body and Soul."

Page 49

Cf. Genesis 3:1–6.

Page 51

L. 14. Cf. Genesis 3:15.

Page 53

Ll. 1–2. Cf. Genesis 3:12–13.

Page 55

L. 8. Cf. Matthew 13:45–46.

Page 59

Ll. 1–4. Cf. Exodus 3:2.

Page 61

Ll. 1–4. The myth of Narcissus, a young man who pined away because he loved his own elusive image.

Ll. 5–10. Cf. Romans 3:20.

Page 69

Ll. 1–2. Cf. II Samuel 24:13.

Ll. 3–4. These lines refer to the suffering caused by the wars against the Spanish as well as the great plagues prevalent in that period.

Page 71

Ll. 1–4. Cf. II Kings 4:29–37.

Page 75

Ll. 1–2. Revius' word *Permessi* stems from *Permessus*, the spring called the Hippocrene, which flows from the peak of the Helicon.

L. 2. Phoebus: the god of music and poetry, but also the sun-god or god of light (Cf. line 5).

L. 3. Cupid: god of love; Venus: goddess of love and beauty, to whom Revius refers as Dione, who was originally Venus' mother.

L. 7. Pegasus: winged horse, the inspirer of poetry.

L. 9. Cyrrha: near Delphi; a harbor used as a refuge in war by the inhabitants of Krisa.

L. 10. To retain the "double" concept, I have had to eliminate the original Parnassus (mountain of Phoebus-Apollo with its twin peaks) and substitute the well-known concept from "Rock of Ages": the double cure, which saves from guilt and makes one pure.

Page 83

Ll. 1–4. Cf. Matthew 2:11.

Ll. 5–9. Cf. Mark 15:23: "And they gave him to drink wine mingled with myrrh: but he received it not." Spiritually, however, in his crucifixion Christ drank the bitter myrrh-wine to the last drop.

Ll. 9–11. Cf. John 19:39.

Page 85

Cf. Matthew 2:16–18.

Page 87

Stanzas 1 and 3. Cf. Matthew 16:2–3: "He answered and said unto them, When it is evening, ye say, *It will be* fair weather: for the sky is red. And in the morning, *It will be* foul weather to day: for the sky is red and lowring. . . ."

Page 91

L. 4. This is probably a reference to Matthew 16:16–18. The spirit of Peter would be that which acknowledges Christ as the "Son of the living God," the spirit of Simon that which does not. The reference may also be to the "Simony" described in Acts 8:18–24.

Page 93

Cf. John 10:33.

Cf. Matthew 13:54–55.
Cf. Luke 7:37–50.
Ll. 7–8. Cf. Exodus 17:1–7.
L. 9. Cf. Exodus 16:14–15.
L. 10. Cf. Numbers 13:23.
L. 14. Cf. John 6:55.
Cf. John 13:4–16.
Cf. Luke 22:44.
Cf. Luke 22:55–62.
Cf. Matthew 27:25.
Cf. Matthew 27:27–35.
Cf. Numbers 21:5–9 and John 3:14.
L. 5. Cf. Malachi 4:2.
L. 20. Cf. Matthew 13:43.
Four Popes: Leo X (1513–1521), who in 1520 pronounced the ban against Luther; Clement VII (1523–1534); Urban VIII (1623–1644), Revius' contemporary; Paul III (1534–1549), who in 1540 confirmed the Jesuit order.
Four Preachers: These four famous leaders of the Reformation are contrasted with the popes of the previous poem. Where Revius uses the name Philips (Philip Melanchton, closely associated with Luther), I have substituted the name of John Knox, the Scottish reformer.
L. 1. Two spirits: the Anabaptists and the Socinians. The

Anabaptists denied that Christ had assumed human flesh from his mother. (cf. *Dutch Confession of Faith*, Article 18). The Socinians, on the other hand, denied Christ's divinity.

Page 135

This is the first of a series of five epitaphs included in these translations.

Page 145

L. 1. This refers to the seven wise men of ancient Greece.

Page 147

This "Answer" refers to the preceding poem.

Page 149

L. 1. Ignatius of Loyola, founder of the Jesuit order, canonized in 1622.

Ll. 5–6. He is called the soldiers' comrade because he had originally been a captain in the army of Charles V of Spain.

Page 151

Anna Maria van Schuurman was one of the few liberally educated and therefore well-known Dutch ladies of the seventeenth century. She was born in 1607 and was around twenty years old when Revius wrote this sonnet in her honor.

Page 153

This elegy and the two following it (pp. 155 and 157) form numbers 3, 5, and 6 of a series of seven sonnets which Revius wrote on the death of Ernest Casimir, Count of Nassau, killed during military action against the Spanish in 1632.

L. 1. Charon: the mythical ferryman who was thought to ferry the souls of the dead across the River Styx to the underworld.

L. 14. Cf. II Kings 2:11.

Page 155

L. 2. Casimir: see the note accompanying the preceding poem.

Ll. 11–14. Casimir's soul is thought of as a new planet gracing the heavens.

Page 157

L. 1. Casimir: see the notes accompanying the preceding two poems.

L. 9. Casimir was *stadhouder* of Friesland. The position of *stadhouder* is somewhat like that of a governor; the position granted widespread powers in the province.

Page 159

L. 2. Frederick Hendrick: Prince of Orange, youngest son of William of Orange.

Ll. 5–8. Three renowned sculptors of the ancient world.

L. 14. This line refers to the prince's triumphant progress along the Maas River in 1632.

Page 161

L. 2. Prince Frederick Hendrick held the title of Captain-Admiral as well as Captain-General.

L. 5. Brabant: a province under Spanish domination, resisting Prince Frederick Hendrick.

Page 163

The Image: on a medallion.

The Prince: Frederick Hendrick; see the notes accompanying the two preceding poems.

Page 165

L. 1. This is the second and the following sonnet (p. 167) the eighth of a series of elegiac sonnets which Revius wrote for the death of King Gustavus Adolphus of Sweden (1594–1632), killed while defending the Protestant cause in Germany. The "cloud" refers to him as coming from the North. Cf. I Kings 18:44.

L. 10. Eagle: the German emperor, Ferdinand II; Dragon: Philip IV of Spain.

Page 167

L. 1. King Gustavus Adolphus. See the notes accompanying the preceding poem.

Page 169

L. 1. Frederick Hendrick, Prince of Orange. This is the fifth of a series of sonnets Revius wrote to celebrate the Prince's military successes in 1633.

L. 3. It was customary thus to illuminate the towns to celebrate a victory.

BIBLIOGRAPHY

W. A. P. SMIT ON REVIUS

Revius, Jacobus. *Over-Ysselsche Sangen en Dichten*, ed. W. A. P. Smit. 2 vols. Amsterdam: Uitgeversmaatschappij Holland, 1930 and 1935.

This is the excellent definitive edition of Revius' poetry. It is based chiefly on the original editions and manuscripts owned by the Deventer Library.

Smit, W. A. P. *De Dichter Revius*. Amsterdam: Uitgeversmaatschappij Holland, 1928.

This fine historical and critical volume is basic to the study of Revius and his work. The first two chapters treat Revius' relationship to the French renaissance and to his own Dutch antecedents and contemporaries. The third chapter characterizes Revius as man and as poet. The remaining chapters (4–7) present a perceptive analysis and evaluation of all the important poems.

OTHERS ON REVIUS

Arens, J. C. "Bewerkingen van Tertullianus en Andere Vaders in Revius' Gedichten," *Spiegel der Letteren*, 5 (1961), 143–149. Further notes by Arens on Revius' sources appear in the following volumes of *Spiegel der Letteren*: Vol. 7(1963–64), 50–54; Vol. 8(1965), 202–212.

———. "Twee Sonnetten bij Revius en Drummond," *Neophilologus*, 47(1963), 151–153.

———. "Van Puntdicht tot Zedeles: Revius Bewerkt Owen," *De Nieuwe Taalgids*, 55(1962), 42–44. Further notes by Arens on Revius' sources appear in the following volumes of *De Nieuwe Taalgids*: Vol. 55 (1962), 266–268; Vol. 56 (1963), 58, 118, 128, and 334–335; Vol. 58(1965), 166–167, 263–264, and 322.

These enlightening articles indicate and document the sources of many of Revius' poems, especially in *The Greek Anthology*, the church fathers, the epigrams of John Owen, and the poets of the French renaissance.

Meyjes, E. J. W. P. *Jacobus Revius, zijn Leven en Werken*. Amsterdam: Ten Brink and De Vries, 1895.

> This dissertation on Revius deals chiefly with his work as theologian and historian, ending with a sketchy chapter on his poetry.

Stapelkamp, Chr. *Revius-Studiën*. Assen: Van Gorcum, 1954.

> This volume gives detailed and helpful notes on the peculiarities of language in Revius' religious poems.

Ten Harmsel, Henrietta. "Jacobus Revius, Dutch Baroque Poet, *Comparative Literature*, XV(Summer, 1963), 203–215.

> An introductory article on Revius and his poetry, comparing him with other baroque poets.

Van Es, G. A. "Protestantsche Letterkunde in de Eerste Helft der 17de Eeuw," *De Letterkunde van Renaissance en Barok in de Zeventiende Eeuw*. Vol. I. 'S Hertogenbosch: Teulings' Uitgevers-Maatschappij, 1948.

> The chapter "Jacobus Revius" (pp. 165–208) sets Revius briefly in his period and then proceeds to characterize the various types of his poetry and to analyze leading poems. This is Volume IV of the *Geschiedenis van de Letterkunde der Nederlanden*, ed. F. Baur.

Wilterdink, J. B. "John Owen en zijn Invloed op Jeremias de Decker en Revius," *Tijdschrift voor Nederlandse Taalen Letterkunde*, 76(1958), 18–40.

> This article indicates that the Latin epigrams of the Englishman John Owen (1564–1622) form the source of many of Revius' epigrammatic poems.

RELATED CRITICS

ON

METAPHYSICAL POETRY

Brooks, Cleanth. *Modern Poetry and the Tradition*. Chapel Hill: University of North Carolina Press, 1939.

The first section of this book (pp. 1–53) with its treatment of wit in metaphysical poetry is pertinent to Revius' work.

de Morgues, Odette. *Metaphysical, Baroque, and Précieux Poetry*. London: Oxford University Press, 1953.

Chapters II, IV, and V are especially helpful in analyzing the metaphysical elements in Revius' poetry.

Gardner, Helen, ed. *The Metaphysical Poets*. Baltimore: Penguin Books, 1957.

Both the introduction and the selection of English metaphysical poetry in this volume are of inestimable help in studying Revius. Readers can find almost all of my quotations from the metaphysical poets in this volume.

Mazzeo, Joseph Anthony. "A Critique of Some Modern Theories of Metaphysical Poetry," *Modern Philology*, L(November, 1952), 88–96.

This illuminating article stresses especially the importance of "universal correspondences" in metaphysical poetry.

Smith, James. "On Metaphysical Poetry," *Scrutiny*, II(December, 1933), 222–239.

Revius' poems treating the relationships between God, man, and the universe are illuminated by Smith's particularizing of the problem of "the Many and the One" in metaphysical poetry.

Warnke, Frank J. *European Metaphysical Poetry*. New Haven and London: Yale University Press, 1961.

Both for its enlightening and richly documented introduction and for its translations of selected metaphysical poets of Europe, this book will surely become a classic in metaphysical criticism. Mr. Warnke includes six Revius translations (pp. 212–223) in his selections from Dutch poets and characterizes Revius' poetry briefly on pp. 66–68.

White, Helen C. *The Metaphysical Poets*. New York: The Macmillan Company, 1956.

A basic study, which analyzes the intellectual and religious climate, defines metaphysical poetry, and treats the individual metaphysical poets of England.

Aspel, Alexander, and Donald Justice, eds. *Contemporary French Poetry*, postface by Paul Engle. Ann Arbor: University of Michigan Press, 1965.

Frost, Robert. *Complete Poems of Robert Frost: 1949.* New York: Henry Holt and Company, 1949.

INDEX *of Poems*

Henrietta Ten Harmsel is Professor of English at Calvin College. She is the author of *Jane Austen — A Study in Fictional Conventions* and various articles in professional journals. She holds the Ph.D. degree from the University of Michigan.

The manuscript was edited by Ralph Busick. The book was designed by S. R. Tenenbaum. The type face for the text is Linotype Granjon and for display is Garamont; both faces originally cut by Claude Garamond at the end of the 16th Century.

The book is printed on S. D. Warren's Olde Style Antique and bound in Interlaken's cloth and Elephant Hide paper over boards. Manufactured in the United States of America.